Italian Texts and Studies on Religion and Society

Edmondo Lupieri, *General Editor*

Italian religious history has been pivotal to the formation and growth of European and Western civilization and cultures. Unfortunately, many texts which are fundamental for the understanding of its importance have long remained inaccessible to non-Italian readers. Similarly, the exciting developments of Italian scholarship in the field of the studies of religion have not always come into the public eye outside of Italy. Particularly since the end of World War II there has been continuous expansion in the field, and currently Italian scholars are combining the old and solid Italian tradition of philological and historical studies with new and innovative ideas and methodologies.

Italian Texts and Studies on Religion and Society (ITSORS) is a new series. Its publications are all English translations of works originally published or composed in Italy. The main aim of ITSORS is to have readers in the English-speaking world become acquainted with Italian socio-religious history and with the best of Italian scholarly research on religion with socio-historical implications. For this reason ITSORS will have two branches: *Texts* and *Studies*.

Texts consist of classical works and are intended to be useful as sources for a better comprehension of important events in Western religious history. Many are not readily available or have never been translated into English. *Studies* comprise original works of the best contemporary Italian scholarship which offer methodological contributions to research and make inroads into seldom studied areas.

ITALIAN TEXTS
& STUDIES
ON RELIGION
& SOCIETY

BOOKS AVAILABLE

Odoric of Pordenone
The Travels of Friar Odoric
(Sponsored by the Chamber of Commerce of Pordenone, Italy)

Edmondo Lupieri
The Mandaeans: The Last Gnostics
(Sponsored by the Italian Ministry of Foreign Affairs)

THE TRAVELS
OF FRIAR ODORIC

Blessed Odoric of Pordenone

Translated by
Sir Henry Yule

WILLIAM B. EERDMANS PUBLISHING COMPANY
GRAND RAPIDS, MICHIGAN / CAMBRIDGE, U.K.

Wm. B. Eerdmans Publishing Co.
255 Jefferson Ave. S.E., Grand Rapids, Michigan 49503 /
P.O. Box 163, Cambridge CB3 9PU U.K.
www.eerdmans.com

Printed in the United States of America

06 05 04 03 02   7 6 5 4 3 2 1

Library of Congress Cataloging-in-Publication Data

Odorico, da Pordenone, 1265?–1331.
[Relatio. English]
The travels of Friar Odoric / Odoric of Pordenone.
p.   cm.   — (Italian texts and studies on religion and society)
Translation by Sir Henry Yule.
Includes bibliographical references (p.   ).
ISBN 0-8028-4963-6 (cloth: alk. paper)
1. Asia — Description and travel — Early works to 1800.
2. China — Description and travel — Early works to 1800.
3. Odorico, da Pordenone, 1265?–1331 — Journeys — Asia.
I. Yule, Henry, Sir, 1820–1889.   II. Title.   III. Series.

DS6.O34137   2002
950'.2 — dc21   2001053857

Stampato con il contributo della Camera di Commercio I.A.A. di Pordenone.
Printed with the contribution of the Camera di Commercio I.A.A. of Pordenone.

CONTENTS

FOREWORD

As one reflects on the life of Blessed Odoric of Pordenone, the question immediately arises: what message can people in our times gather from this individual?

Reading his *Relatio,* we learn about many of the strange customs and things that Odoric observed while amongst the people he encountered on the road. But more than this, he conveys two virtues that are especially helpful for today: great humility and respect for one's neighbor. His Franciscan style of humility shows itself in the fact that, because of his deep faith in Christ, he withstood great hardships and overcame difficulties without boasting about it. Moreover, Odoric was an observer who respected the customs and traditions of an unknown world, with a spontaneous tolerance for religions different from his.

Odoric was a humble son of Saint Francis who, in imitation of his seraphic Father, embraced all peoples.

The Commission for the Canonization and Veneration of Blessed Odoric of Pordenone works to further the spread of his cult and to create a new awareness of this great and holy Friulian pioneer. The Commission is, therefore, pleased to present this new English edition of the *Relatio.* We would also like to profoundly thank Professor Edmondo Lupieri for his work as editor, Professor Paolo Chiesa for the extensive and well-documented introduction, and the Chambers of Commerce, Industry, Handicrafts, and Agriculture of Pordenone for their generous sponsorship. A special mention goes to the staff of William B. Eerdmans Publishing Company for their diligence in preparing this publication and for their contribution to the body of knowledge concerning the heroic missionary figure, Odoric. They have greatly facilitated the work of those doing study and research in this field, as well as those who use English to establish economic, social, and cultural ties, as well as bonds of peace and friendship, with brother populations. Among these peoples we would especially like to mention the immense Chinese population, evangelized by Odoric.

July 16th, A.D. 2000

Signature,
Antonio Vitale Bommarco, O.F.M, Conv.
Archbishop,
President of the Commission for the
Canonization and Veneration of
Blessed Odoric of Pordenone
The Archbishop's Seal:
Antonio Vitale Bommarco
Archbishop Emeritus of Gorizia

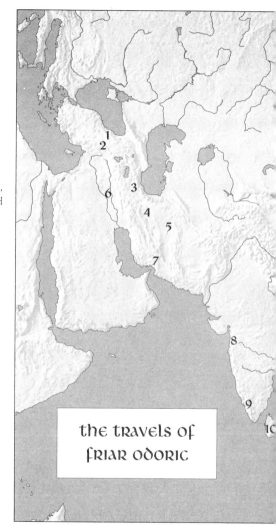

the travels of
friar odoric

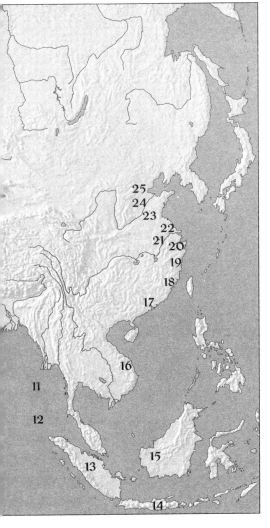

INTRODUCTION

Paolo Chiesa

"When we found ourselves amongst these people, it seemed like we had entered into another world." William of Rubruck, one of many western travellers on the roads to the East in the last centuries of the Middle Ages, used these simple but extremely concise words to describe his first contact with the Mongols. His explorations, like those of many before and after him, were adventurous and were motivated by commercial, political, religious, and military factors. Those who, in fact, returned to Europe from eastern travels — and not all did — carried with them a rich collection of news, surprises, and wonders. They narrated these wonders to their friends and fellow brothers, and these tales were sometimes written down as marvellous descriptions of a fantastic world. This book speaks of one of these men and the stories that he told and had others write down.

Odoric of Pordenone died on the thirteenth of January, 1331, in the Franciscan monastery of Udine, a city about 100 kilometers northeast of Venice. During his life, he was renowned for his holiness. The public magistrate, apparently in opposition to the wishes of the deceased's superiors, ordered a public funeral, and the body was displayed for public veneration. The bishop's sister, who had long suffered from paralysis in her arm, suddenly shouted out that she had been cured by merely touching the remains of Odoric. In the resultant chaos, the rumor spread that a woman had tried to cut off a finger of the dead man to keep as an amulet. Though she was not successful, having been stopped by a mysterious, invisible power, authorities locked the body in a reliquary to avoid public upheaval and to protect the corpse. Days later, when they opened the reliquary in order to put Odoric in his permanent burial place, the corpse was still intact and manifested all the signs of sanctity: it emitted a heavenly odor, the face had a peaceful appearance, the body itself was still supple to the touch, and the blood remained liquid in the veins.

At the end of May of the same year, 1331, less than

five months after Odoric's death, the patriarch of
Aquileia, Pagano della Torre, whose bishopric included
the territory of Udine, commissioned an investigation
of the miracles that were said to be continuing at
Odoric's tomb. The commission was convened by
Corrado of Bernareggio, who was the chamberlain and
chief administrator of the city of Udine. Also partici-
pating was a notary by the name of Guecello, a priest,
the rector Melioranza, and a civilian of the city, Maffeo
Cassini. For two months they searched far and wide in
the region, collecting testimony pertaining to approximately seventy miracles, almost all of which were miraculous recoveries occurring at the tomb of the friar or
through his intercession. The purpose of the investigation was obviously to initiate proceedings for the beatification of Odoric. The undertaking did not meet with
success, however. Patriarch Pagano died in 1332, and the
Franciscans apparently did not pursue the initiative very
energetically.

This, together with other factors, might lead one to
believe that Odoric was not particularly liked within the
Order; perhaps this was because of the severity of his
highly moral life and his rigorous poverty. After all, these
were very difficult times for the Franciscans. Between 1328

and 1330, the highest authority of the Order, the father superior, Michele of Cesena, had openly supported the antipope Nicholas V, born Peter of Corbara, who was himself a Franciscan. Nicholas V had been named pope by the emperor, Louis the Bavarian, in opposition to the Avignon pope, John XXII. The schism ended with Pope John's victory, and the Franciscans, although officially pardoned, continued to be viewed with some suspicion. At the same time, a debate over poverty continued within the Order, a debate that had caused serious divisions in past years. After numerous clashes, sometimes violent, the moderate wing had prevailed over the more spiritually severe, who were officially condemned in the years 1317-18. However, the matter continued to be a source of unrest. Consequently, with the death of Pagano, the process of Odoric's beatification was delayed, and further miraculous events were not recorded. Only in 1755, after new canonical proceedings, was Odoric beatified by Pope Benedict XIV.

The events surrounding Odoric's burial and the alleged miracles attributed to his corpse were recorded in the *Chronica XXIV Generalium Ordinis Minorum,* one of the main sources for the early history of the Franciscan Order. This chronicle, taken from the report of the notary Guecello, was written about forty years after the fact and has been handed down to us in two manuscripts from the late Middle Ages. Odoric's fame as a saint developed not only because his lifestyle was presumed to have been marked by great virtue but especially as a result of the extraordinary voyage he made in the faraway and dangerous lands of the East.

We know little else about him. The *Chronica* refers, rather briefly, to his activities before his travels, in very common terms that seem to follow the usual hagiographic truisms. Odoric appears to have become a friar at a very early age and to have led a life characterized by strict ascesis. It seems that he loathed rank and honor, and he retreated for a time to a hermitage. Miraculous healings were attributed to him while he was still alive. In the Franciscan church in Udine, two chains were displayed at the end of the fourteenth century as instruments of penitence belonging to Odoric, with which he was said to have bound up his body and arms.

The sources agree that Odoric was born in Pordenone, a small city on the Friuli plain, about sixty kilometers from Venice. More difficult to ascertain is whether he was, in fact, the son of a soldier serving in the retinue of the king of Bohemia, Ottakar II, who fought successfully for control of Pordenone in 1269-70. Because of this tradition, Odoric was sometimes called "the Bohemian." Another tradition, not well founded, says instead that he belonged to an old local family and that there is still a house today in the suburbs of Pordenone identified as his. Nothing is known of the date of his birth; it could have taken place any time between 1265 and 1285. Two Austrian manuscripts describe Odoric like this: "He was small of stature because of the severity of his asceticism, with a pallid face and a long, reddish, forked beard, which contained some streaks of white. He led a holy life, full of prayer, and he was soft-spoken and humble in what he said." The forked beard, which seems to have been the most characteristic part of his appearance, also shows up in two portraits of Odoric appearing on two bas-reliefs that decorate his tomb. These works were done immediately after his death by the Venetian sculptor Filippo de Santis and are now located in the church of Our Lady of Carmel in Udine.

Odoric's reputation for saintliness during his lifetime was established not so much by his ascetic habits as by his extraordinary journey. These travels made him a hero and bestowed on him the reputation of having an aura of divine protection. It was believed that his return to the West was prompted, not by the need for rest after a tiring mission, but rather by his desire to expand the evangelization of the East by recruiting other companions with whom to set out again. A legend that spread after his death expresses well the popular opinion of him as a man totally dedicated to this mission and as one protected by God. It is said that, at the end of 1330, Odoric set out from either Padua or Udine toward Avignon, where the pope was stationed at that time, to ask the pontiff for some companions to send to the East with him, in order to make his missionary work there more effective. But on the journey, before he had gotten as far as Pisa, he was miraculously warned of his impending death. Legend has it that Odoric met an old man along the road who was dressed in pilgrim's clothes and who greeted him by name. He was surprised and asked the man how he knew his name. The old man answered that he had known him for a long while, from the time of Odoric's mission in Asia. The stranger then advised him to return to his monastery in Udine because he was going to die ten days later. Odoric did as he was told and went back to Udine. There he died peacefully, as predicted. This legend, which is found in a dense group of manuscripts in the *Relatio,* is also retold in the *Chronica XXIV Generalium,* but with some modifications to make Odoric fit well into the perspective of the Franciscans. For example, according to the *Chronica,* Odoric was going to Avignon not to procure new missionaries but to pray for his Order, which was undergoing many ordeals. The figure that appeared to him was not an old pilgrim (an angel?) but Saint Francis himself, surrounded by a cloud "bright in the center and dark outside." He was ordered to die in Udine because the city of Pisa was not worthy of keeping his remains, having been responsible for the arrest of the antipope Nicholas V.

The description of Odoric's journey to the East comes to us from the account that he made on returning. It was most likely dictated or narrated by him, rather than being written in his own hand. In this book, we will call the report the *Relatio,* at that time a traditional name, but certainly different from the title that it originally had. The original name is difficult to reconstruct. We know that in May of 1330 Odoric might have already returned to Italy when his fellow friar, William of Solagna, compiled and underwrote an edition of the *Relatio* in the Franciscan monastery of Padua. But it is not exactly clear when he departed. According to some sources, the trip lasted fourteen and a half years and started in the fall of 1315, at the latest; according to other sources it lasted twelve or sixteen years and therefore began in either 1314 or 1318. A notary document of 1317 lists as a witness a certain *frater Odorlicus de Portunaonis,* who can mostly likely be identified with our friar. It is not inconceivable that two monks had the same name (the name Odoric was very common in Pordenone). Excluding this possibility, however, we may conclude that his departure would have taken place after 1317. As indicated, it is most likely that his return to Italy in 1330 was thought to be only temporary and that he planned to leave soon after for the East.

Odoric certainly left from Venice, stopping in Constantinople, where he stayed at the Franciscan monastery in the northern suburb of Pera. In the majority of manuscripts of the *Relatio,* his travels begin from here; the trip from Venice to Constantinople was considered only a preparatory leg of the journey. He headed by sea for Trebizond (today's Trabzon) along the Anatolian coast of the Black Sea. From there he continued by land, following the caravan route that led southeast. He passed through Arziron (Erzurum), Tauris (Tabriz), Soldania (Soltaniyeh), and Cassan (Kashan), along the direct route across Kurdistan and the Iranian plateau, until he arrived at Iest (Yazd), located about five hundred kilometers southeast of Teheran.

At this point, the *Relatio* cites some sources that seem to indicate a long digression west, as far as Mesopotamia, a fact that puzzled the commentators. Such a change in direction would be completely illogical during a trip that was destined for India and China, but, as will be noted later, Odoric did not seem to be in a hurry. Also, it is unlikely that he had a very precise travel plan. If we allow for some confusion in the recording of the different stops, which is very possible, Odoric would have reached Mesopotamia, not by way of distant Iest, but by way of Soldania, which was closer. Lucio Monaco theorizes that, in this case, the monk would have been able to take part in the missionary expedition organized by the little Franciscan community situated in that city. It is very unlikely that Odoric confused his memories here with those of some previous trip in the Holy Land and the Middle East. It also seems inadvisable to suppose that he was recounting here things that he had heard from others, without ever being in the area. Therefore, a detour into Mesopotamia seems possible, at least.

Directly from Iest, or from Mesopotamia (in the latter case, he would have followed a route parallel to the coast and along a road that was as frequently travelled as the more northerly one going to Soldania and Cassan), he finally reached Ormes (Hormuz, modern Bandar-Abbas), the arrival point for trans-Iranian caravans. From there he set off along the route that led to the East. His first important stop was Tana, near modern Bombay, where he recovered the relics of four Franciscan friars executed by the Muslims in April of 1321. His passage through Tana, therefore, must have taken place after that date. The journey progressed along the west coast of India to Polumbum (Quilon), near the southern tip of the Indian peninsula. From there, the information in the *Relatio* is confused; among the localities mentioned, in an inconsistent order, there is the island of Ceylon (called Silan by Odoric), Coromandel (Mobar), the Nicobar Islands (Nicoveran), perhaps the Andaman Islands (if one of these can be identified as the island which he referred to as Dondin), Sumatra (Sumoltra), Java, possibly Borneo (Panten), finishing with the kingdom of Zampa, found on the southern coast of Vietnam. Apart from some geographic incongruities, the itinerary followed was evidently the maritime one through the Gulf of Bengal and the Strait of Malacca. His route becomes consistent again once he embarks from the kingdom of Manzi, in southern China, along a route that led to the city of Censcalan (modern Guangzhou [Canton]). From there, he travelled by land or by sea to the other big coastal cities, such as Zayton (a place not exactly identifiable but probably not far from Zhangzhou [Amoy]), Fuzo (Fuzhou), and Cansay (Hangzhou). Then he moved to the kingdom of Cathay — namely, northern China — along an internal route that took him to Chilenfu (Nanjing) [Nanking]), Lenzin (probably Linqing), and Sunzumayu (most likely Jining). Finally, he arrived at Cambalech, which is today Beijing (Peking), headquarters of the Great Khan. He stayed in the imperial capital for three years, probably from 1324 to 1327.

The *Relatio* is not explicit about Odoric's return trip. The final chapters, which come after the description of the Khan's imperial court, appear very disorganized with regard to geographic order and do not allow us to reconstruct his itinerary. Odoric refers (in chapter 43) to the incredible birth of vegetable lambs; he did not personally witness this event, but said that it was described to him by a very trustworthy person. The location seems to have been in the Caucasus Mountains. Then there is a narration (chapter 44) of the land of Prester John, a region identified by the commentators, somewhat uncertainly, as central Mongolia. Next, the *Relatio* speaks about Shaanxi and then Tibet (chapter 45). Chapters 46 and 47 tell us about two legends, the location of which is not exactly certain: the legend of the rich man fed by his maids, and the legend of the Old Man of the Mountain. Chapter 48 is concerned with the great power of the Franciscans in Tartary in casting out demons; chapter 49 tells of Odoric's visit to the infernal valley, which the commentators tend to associate, without convincing evidence, with the Hindu Kush Mountains. Chapter 51, which is not part of the first version of the *Relatio*, refers back to an episode that happened during Odoric's stay in Cambalech, in which the Franciscans gave their blessing to the Great Khan himself. The fact that chapters concerning Prester John, Shaanxi, and Tibet follow consecutively makes us think that Odoric's return trip was by land, but there is no real proof of this.

Odoric's motives for the voyage seem to have been exclusively missionary in nature: "I crossed the sea and visited the countries of the unbelievers in order to win some harvest of souls," says Odoric in the preface to the *Relatio*. And at no point in the account did he act in the capacity of ambassador or diplomat. The goal of gaining souls may not have been preordained, and this could explain some of the apparent contradictions in the itinerary that followed; the travel schedule might have been modified according to needs and circumstances. Odoric is the only religious traveller to the East whose voyage is recorded, yet it does not appear that he was sent by an official organization. It is true that the *Relatio* mentions Guidotto of Bassano, who was the provincial superior of the Franciscans in Padua and in direct authority over Odoric. But Guidotto's role could have been limited to asking for a travel report, without his being in any way the instigator of the trip; furthermore, a provincial superior was not in a high enough position to give full authorization for such an enterprise. Henry of Glarus, a Bohemian Franciscan who rewrote the *Relatio* immediately after Odoric's death, seemingly felt somewhat uneasy when considering the apparent spontaneity of Odoric's journey and thought it necessary to clarify that it was undertaken "with the permission of his superiors, who could sanction an enterprise of this sort, according to what the rules of the Order say." Therefore, Odoric's journey was not an official assignment, but rather a personal initiative that received the necessary authorization. If we are to believe the story, the decision to retrieve the relics of the brothers who had suffered martyrdom and to transfer them to a Christian monastery, in order to give them an honorary burial, was a dangerous one. But it was a decision that was very much in keeping with the picture of the generous and nonconformist friar that the *Relatio* gives us of Odoric.

Odoric travelled with a companion and a servant, but the names of these two people are not given, and they are mentioned only once. It is very possible that his companion can be identified as an Irish monk, a certain James of Ibernia, who assisted at Odoric's funeral in Udine and subsequently received a subsidy from the city. To him is owed the strange account of the trees in Ireland that give birth to birds spontaneously (chapter 43).

Along the way, Odoric indicated the presence of Christian communities and of Franciscan settlements; he enjoyed the hospitality of the latter whenever possible. Odoric almost always took pains to note the religious customs of the places he visited; his attitude toward these customs is often curiosity and tolerance. His condemnation appears to have fallen above all on the historical enemies of Roman Catholicism: the Muslims (or "Saracens") and the Nestorian Christians.

The journey of Odoric, like his life, was soon the object of reexamination in a hagiographic light. The *Chronica XXIV Generalium,* which is a somewhat official text, recounts only a small portion of the stories narrated in the *Relatio,* yet adds others to demonstrate Odoric's sanctity while he was still alive. For example, it is reported that the friar fell seriously ill in a land where no one was allowed to lodge a Christian, the punishment for doing so being the death penalty and the confiscation of all possessions. A farmer placed him, as best he could, under a tree, and Odoric lived there for an entire year, eating the fruit of the same tree and drinking the liquid that flowed from the trunk. On another occasion, Odoric ate a miraculous fruit that he had found in a watercourse, and this was enough to sustain him for nine days. It is told that the Virgin Mary appeared to Odoric and directed him to bring the Eucharist to a holy lady who was near death; this story is so detailed that one suspects Odoric himself as the source. Of those episodes recorded in the *Relatio,* the *Chronica* takes up and narrates only the final ones, those in which the elements of miracles are most evident: the power of the Franciscans in China in driving away demons; Odoric's visit to, and survival of, the infernal valley; and his blessing of the Great Khan. Finally, we are told of another episode that occurred on his mysterious return trip. The *Chronica* states that Odoric's return was necessary to recruit new missionaries in order to keep up the evangelization of the East. Along the road, he came across the devil, in the disguise of a woman, who told him of his firm opposition to the plan and informed him, at the same time, that he would never return to that land. Present at this encounter (though incapable of distinguishing the demon) was his travelling companion, who began to wonder about the friar's sanity after hearing him speaking to himself.

Odoric's journey, however peculiar and, in certain respects, "anarchical" it may be, became in fact part of a rich travelling tradition that brought many European clerics to the East. These expeditions generally combined spiritual intentions (that is, the conversion of pagan peoples) with more earthly aims, particularly those of a diplomatic and exploratory nature.

In the fall of 1237, the papal legate to Hungary received a letter from a Dominican brother by the name of Julian, who in previous years had been the leader of two evangelistic missions in the region between the Urals and Kazakhstan. In this passionately written letter, Julian did his best to warn Christianity of the serious and unknown danger that was threatening it: invasion by the Mongols, a fierce and powerful people whom Brother Julian had seen in action in the territories he had visited and who he knew were marching toward Europe. Brother Julian wrote:

While we were heading for our destination, and had already reached the outer boundaries of Russia, we learned of something unexpected and surprising: all of the pagan Hungarians and Bulgarians, who lived in that zone, had been destroyed and subjected to the Mongols, and also, many other kingdoms. . . . We stopped, therefore, at the border of Russia; here we learned that the Mongols have divided their army into four groups, and that they are heading for various regions of Russia. From what the refugees report, they are waiting for winter to freeze the swamps and rivers, in order to more easily conquer, and sack, Russia and Ruthenia. . . . Those who are well informed state that the Mongols discuss, day and night, how to defeat the Christian kingdom of Hungary, and rule over it; their real plan is to arrive in Rome, conquer her, and continue on from there.

The danger of invasion, at that moment, was very real. Mongol expansion, which up to that point had been limited to Asiatic regions, saw a major acceleration, beginning in 1236. Between 1237 and 1238, the Mongols pillaged the majority of Russian principalities, going as far as Susdal, Moscow, and Vladimir; in 1240, they destroyed Kiev, the religious metropolis of the Russian world. In 1241, they burned Cracow and devastated Poland and Silesia, annihilating a Christian army sent to stop them. They flooded into Bohemia and Moravia, from there descending into Hungary, where they destroyed Pest, after which they chased King Bela IV up to the boundary of Italy and the Adriatic. In a period of five years, the Mongols earned a reputation for being invincible and merciless warriors, spreading terror everywhere and evoking the name of the diabolical people of Gog and Magog. No one seemed capable of halting them. Then, at the end of 1241, they hurried away, as suddenly and inexplicably as they had arrived. Today we know that they were called back to their homeland in order to participate in the election of the new Khan, who was to replace the deceased Ogodei.

Their retreat, which was proclaimed a miracle, gave the West the chance to prepare for any possible future raids; to accomplish this, however, much information about the strength and organization of the enemy was needed. It was also necessary to look into the feasibility of entering into an alliance with them, perhaps one that could operate against the Muslims; if not, at least a truce could be negotiated. All of this would require the opening of both cultural and diplomatic relations with the newcomers. Some official expeditions of western clerics to China were connected to this type of necessity much more than to the need to expand missionary activity; these expeditions were organized with the support of the pope and entrusted primarily to Franciscan friars.

The first missions were organized in 1245 by Pope Innocent IV and were placed in the hands of the Franciscan John of Plano Carpini and the Dominicans Andrew of Longjumeau and Ascelino of Cremona. John left from Lyons and arrived at the court of the Great Khan at Karakorum, in northern Mongolia, after more than a year of travel across Poland, Russia, Kazakhstan, and the Central Asian plateau. After some months, he set out again for Europe, which he reached at the end of 1247, carrying with him a letter from the Mongolian sovereign and an interesting account known as the *Historia Tartarorum.* This report describes both the journey and, through the eyes of the explorer, the habits of the Mongols, especially the military customs, which interested western leaders the most. We receive other information about the trip from two of John's companions, Benedict of Poland and someone identified only as C. of Bridia, both of whom left independent reports. Less is known of the other two expeditions, which had to deal with the more complex political situation and hostility of the Muslim principalities. Andrew of Longjumeau left from Jerusalem and pushed on, with great difficulty, as far as Tabriz, on the Iranian plateau; no written account of his travels is left. Ascelino of Cremona left from Constantinople and ventured into the

Caucasus Mountains, reaching the encampment of the Khan of the Persian Mongols and returning home in 1248; only a part of his travel account remains, written by his partner, Simon of Saint-Quentin.

A subsequent mission, this time organized by Louis IX of France, began in 1252, led by the Flemish Franciscan William of Rubruck. He left from Constantinople, made a stop in the Crimea, and from there continued across Kazakhstan, along a slightly more southerly route than that of John of Plano Carpini. After stopping to visit the Mongol princes of western Asia, William finally arrived at the court of the Great Khan, where he stayed for some months, between 1253 and 1254. He returned home by way of the Caucasus Mountains and Armenia. Once in Europe, he wrote a long report of the trip, which constitutes one of the most lively and interesting documents of thirteenth-century literature. In his report William shows himself to be an excellent observer and a great narrator, and he is very good at transmitting to the reader the feelings and emotions experienced en route. Unlike John, who employed a simple and descriptive style, William knows how to personalize the story and enrich it with the anecdotes of a traveller. William gives a great deal of valuable and interesting information about Mongolian customs and habits, describing their habitations, clothing, food, drink, handicrafts, sicknesses, religious rituals, laws, and burials; the account, beyond being an important literary text, is a historical and ethnographic document of great value. In spite of this, William's *Itinerarium* was not very popular in its day; we know of only five manuscripts, which suggests that it had very limited circulation among his contemporaries.

The Mongols did not enter Europe again after the large invasion from 1236 to 1241, though there was one exception a century and a half later when, in 1396, Tamerlane's Mongols were able to set foot in Kiev again for a brief period. The great empire that Genghis Khan created at the beginning of the 1200s progressively weakened after 1260, and the focus of interest for the empire's rulers shifted decisively toward China, leaving behind the too-distant lands of the West. The empire's capital was transferred from Karakorum to Cambalech — that is, from Outer Mongolia to Cathay. In this situation, the urgency for missions of an exploratory, diplomatic, or military nature diminished. The decrease in tensions and the more serene political environment favored the intermingling of diverse commercial activities, while more space was left for projects that had less immediate but wider aims, namely those concentrating on the evangelization of the East.

The journeys of the Polo family are set in this new context. The two brothers Niccolò and Maffeo Polo, Venetian merchants, departed from Constantinople around 1260-61, spurred on by the potential for profit and the acquisition of precious goods. They reached Cambalech in 1265, where they received the warmest possible welcome from the Great Khan, Qubilai. The sovereign entrusted them with a letter for the pope. They reentered Italy in 1269, deciding shortly afterward to set off for the East a second time. In 1271 they left the Holy Land, heading directly for the court of the Great Khan and carrying a letter of response from the pontiff. This time they brought with them Niccolò's seventeen-year-old son, Marco. The three travellers returned to Venice in 1295, after a trip as exciting and fantastic as ever there was.

Their travels were detailed by Marco in the *Livre des merveilles du monde*, probably better known by its Italian title, *Milione*. After reaching Cambalech by land, via Persia and Pamir, the three Italian merchants entered into the Khan's favor to such an extent that they were awarded the highest recognitions and earned his total trust. The young Marco, in particular, was charged with various assignments as an inspector in diverse and remote regions of the empire; these took him to Tibet, Burma, and Indochina. He accomplished his tasks so well that he was rewarded with the governorship of the city of Yangzhou, north of Nanking. In 1292 they decided to return home because they had been asked to escort a royal princess to Persia, where she was to marry a local ruler. This time they travelled by sea; they went through Indochina, Sumatra, the Nicobar Islands, and the Andaman Islands, then along the Indian coast, as far as Bandar-Abbas; from there, they brought the princess to the Persian court. The Polos remained there for some months, after which they continued on, across the Iranian plateau, to Trabzon, where they embarked for Constantinople and Venice. Marco Polo's powers of observation, his narrative ability, and the vastness and variety of the experiences he lived through all made his travel account the most celebrated of this type of literature. It had immediate success, with copies circulating by the dozens in all of Europe.

Along with the commercial activities of merchants, there were also missionary efforts. In 1294, the Italian Franciscan John of Montecorvino arrived in Cambalech; he had been sent east by Pope Nicholas IV. He had left from Antioch and had followed the Iranian road through

Tabriz, Soltaniyeh, and Bandar-Abbas, and then had taken the sea route for Quilon and the coast of Coromandel. Here his travelling companion, Brother Nicholas of Pistola, died, and he continued along as far as China with a merchant, Peter of Lucalongo. He received a warm welcome at Cambalech and established a Catholic church there, of which he became the first bishop. The letters he wrote to the West insisted that there was a good possibility of evangelizing China; for this reason, the next pope, Clement V, sent a new support mission, which reached Peking in 1308 after a lot of hardships. Thanks to the new clerics (Gerard Albuini, Pellegrino of Città di Castello, and Andrew of Perugia), a new bishopric was founded in Zayton, which was subordinate to the one in Peking, and its missionary work seemed destined to develop positively. Odoric stayed for a time in Cambalech while John of Montecorvino was still bishop there, and it seemed to him, too, that the mission would continue to grow. As a matter of fact, evangelistic activity in China was very fragile, hanging on to the West, as it were, by a mere thread; the ecclesiastics present in both Cambalech and Zayton were all western, and they had no plans to develop a local clergy. Substitute religious personnel came from Europe, meaning that they had to undergo all the risks and potential accidents of a trip that was never easy, and not always successful. Difficulties arose for the first time right after the death of John of Montecorvino (1328) and of those who had travelled to China with him (the last survivor, Andrew, probably died in 1332); the bishop's see in Cambalech remained vacant for a number of years and was not to be occupied in a stable manner until 1342. In that year, the Florentine Franciscan John of Marignola was sent to Cambalech by Pope Benedict XII, accompanied by a group of about fifty missionaries. They travelled by land: departing from Naples, they passed through Constantinople, the Crimea, and Kazakhstan, and finally arrived in Cambalech after skirting the Gobi Desert. Three or four years later, this same group, including John, reentered the West, having travelled by sea through the Strait of Malacca and Bandar-Abbas; from there, they had taken a southerly route through Baghdad, Mosul, and Damascus to their final destination, Jerusalem.

Because of the abundance of men and goods involved, John of Marignola's expedition was the most challenging of those that were sent to China from the West in the course of the Middle Ages; but it was also special in that it was the last of such trips. After this period, we know nothing more of the successive bishops of Cambalech, such as William of Pre, who was commissioned in 1370 by Pope Urban V to go east, together with other companions; we really do not even know if they ever arrived at their new see. Beginning in the middle of the fourteenth century, the political situation became less favorable to such journeys and missions. The weakening of Mongol power allowed the Muslim principalities to resume their ventures into western Asia; generally, they were hostile to the passage of merchants and Christian missionaries through their region. Such difficulties became even greater in central Asia, where the Mongolian Yuan dynasty had left their dominions to the autochthonous Ming, which had caused the Chinese empire to shift its axis of interest definitively toward the Pacific. As a result, the main roads leading to the East had become very unsafe.

In 1340, the Florentine merchant Francesco Balducci Pegolotti wrote a strange but interesting guide for his colleagues who wanted to go to China, a guide that was destined not to be used for long. Francesco advised merchants to let their beards grow, to hire an interpreter without worrying about the cost, to bring a woman with them in order to be treated with greater respect and less diffidence, and to stock up on fish and flour before leaving; these foodstuffs were difficult to find on the road, unlike meat.

But above all he emphasized that the land course between the Black Sea and Cambalech, notwithstanding its length (about three hundred days of travel), was absolutely safe for a caravan of normal dimensions. There were only two real dangers to face on the road: the first presented itself if a merchant died, in which case the Mongols were authorized to confiscate the goods of his fellow travellers; the second was if the Khan died, which could lead to a period of anarchy. But this state of affairs lasted for only a dozen years; after this period, and for centuries to come, the central Asian caravan routes would fall into abandon, as did the sea routes through the Straits of Hormuz and Malacca.

Some of the reports of the travellers who went to the East became remarkably popular in the last centuries of the Middle Ages. Odoric's *Relatio* was one of these.

In Odoric's time, travel literature already had a long tradition. The Middle Ages in the West had inherited from classical tradition two models for this literary genre: the first was the scientific model, in which a travel account served as the springboard for geographic or anthropological observations; the second was a fictional model, in which the journey, usually in exotic places, became a means of describing a multiplicity of amazing adventures.

28

To these two models were added the new needs and experiences of Christianity. As a result, a literature of pilgrimage to the Holy Land was born, these particular pilgrimages having been very popular ever since the last centuries of antiquity. This type of writing combined the actual description of the trip with technical indications given to make the journey easier for the faithful. Still, up until the 1200s, the geographic horizon of the traveller had been limited to Palestine and the other Arab countries. Yet this did not mean that the pilgrims' stories were any less adventurous, and they also confirmed the information and observations that already belonged to medieval Europe's wealth of knowledge and imagination.

The Far East, on the other hand, was still an unknown in the medieval world. After the interruption of caravan travel to the Far East following the Arabic conquest, and because of the progressive limitations on the West's economic resources, travellers and merchants had for centuries no longer taken the routes that led beyond Syria and the Caucasus region. What lay on the other side was a mystery, belonging to the realm of the unreal.

A question that the Europeans did not know how to answer regarded the Christianization of the East. It was said that these lands had been consecrated with the blood of the apostles (according to apocryphal tradition, Thomas, Bartholomew, Andrew, Matthias, and Philip had conducted their missions in India and had there suffered martyrdom), and the tomb of the disciple Thomas was believed to be preserved on the southeast coast of India. There was also a widespread legend that a very powerful Christian sovereign named Prester John controlled a rich and vast territory in the East, near Islamic lands. A letter attributed to him circulated through all of Europe beginning in the second half of the twelfth century. It glorified the strength of Prester John's realm, describing its riches and its palaces and enumerating the wonders of his court. This extraordinary ruler, whose invincibility was never questioned, was ready to intervene on behalf of Christianity wherever it may have been in danger. But the letter was a fake, perhaps devised in the entourage of Emperor Frederick "Barbarossa" as propaganda in support of the Crusade. The letter's popularity reveals a desire for knowledge that went beyond mere published documents. Those travellers going to the East knew this legend very well and could not help but be disillusioned. The comforting kingdom of Prester John did not exist: any Christians they found living near the Muslims were members of small, poor Nestorian communities. Odoric himself said, with some embarrassment and without providing precise geographic coordinates, that Prester John's realm existed, but "as regards him not one hundredth part is true of what is told of him as if it were undeniable" (chapter 44).

It was widely believed that great marvels were to be found in the East. According to one interpretation of a controversial passage of the Bible, the wonderful Garden of Eden, where God had placed the first man and woman and which they inhabited until the Fall, could still be found there. It was said that Eden was the source of the four great rivers of the world, generally identified as the Euphrates, the Indus, the Ganges, and the Nile (though the latter makes little geographical sense). From the High Middle Ages on, a popular legend spread about the search for this lost paradise. The legend tells of three monks from a monastery in Mesopotamia who decided to go to the Far East to find the place where the sky touches the ground. Their journey lasted for months and months, and the three passed through Persia before entering into India, where they underwent every type of ordeal: they met men with dog-like heads and also Pygmies; they were attacked by Ethiopians in service to the devil; they had to face dragons, vipers, and basilisks. They crossed dreadful deserts, lands without light, and plains infested with elephants.

Then they came across an arch built by Alexander as a memorial to his victory over Darius, a lake full of damned souls, a giant chained between two mountains, a woman imprisoned by a dragon, a bush where spirits in the shape of birds lived, and finally a very beautiful place, full of the sweetest songs and light perfumes, where a church had been constructed out of what appeared to be colored crystal. Still the explorers carried on, passing through new populations of Pygmies, until at last they reached a cave where they met a holy hermit named Macarius. Here they stopped. The old man told them that it was only twenty miles to the earthly paradise, but that no man was allowed to go any further.

In the medieval imagination, therefore, the East was a place of the supernatural: a place of extreme holiness, but also of terrible ferocity and indescribable ungodliness. Hellenistic novels about Alexander the Great's expeditions in India and the lands and deserts of the East told of monstrous men and animals that inhabited the area; the peoples that they met along the way followed barbaric and inhuman customs. The anthropophagites, who represented an extreme level of moral degradation, lived there, along with people who had the appearance of humans but lived like beasts. There were also sciapodes, who had just one large foot, with which they protected themselves from the scorching sun as they lay on their backs. The expeditions also reported finding women with beards down to their chests, with oxtails, and with camel hooves, and men with gigantic ears that they wrapped around themselves to keep warm at night.

Odoric, too, discovered anthropophagites and reported encountering peoples with bestial habits such as necrophagy, which was practiced in Tibet. He saw or heard of monstrous men, cynocephaluses, women with feral teeth, and Pygmies. Although some of these seemed hardly human, Odoric observed that "they have rational souls like ourselves." He had heard, too, of the painful deformations that struck the men of Chaldea, whose testicles were stretched out excessively, due to the heat, and who strove to tie them up to their waists so they would not drag on the ground. Though many of these stories seem quite fantastic, in comparison to the literature of preceding centuries this was a new era: geographic horizons had changed, and the new imagery that Europe began to create about the East was now based more and more on direct observation.

These, then, were the expectations and the background with which western merchants and missionaries set off for the East. Such traditions, no matter how fictional, formed a backdrop of anticipation that was impossible to disregard. What were the Europeans searching for in the outer reaches of Asia? And what did they see and not see? Odoric's *Relatio* gives us a good example of the observations of a European voyager, and it can be read from various perspectives and dimensions.

The first dimension, directly tied to Odoric's monastic situation and to the evangelistic reasons for his travels — not to mention the importance of religion in the Middle Ages — is naturally the spiritual one. Although the *Relatio* states that Odoric left for the East with the goal of winning over souls, there is no mention of any conversions that he made. One cannot doubt, however, that he did, in fact, obtain converts, even if the figure given in the *Chronica XXIV Generalium* of the twenty thousand baptisms he performed is certainly exaggerated. The silence surrounding his missionary activity could fall within the more general attitude of humility that was asked of Franciscans, even if not always followed. This fits well with what is known of Odoric's character. Probably, the conversions were made by others: the martyred friars of Tana who with their deaths demonstrated the excellence of the faith they professed; or the Franciscan community of Cansay that had converted the rich man who, later, would show Odoric the garden of metempsychosis, a place both ridiculous and extraordinary.

There is one important exception to the silence in the *Relatio* concerning Odoric's evangelistic activities. The episode is suspect in part because of its position; it is placed at the end of the work, when Odoric should already have been on his return trip, but it speaks of an event set in the court of the Great Khan, which he had actually left some time before. It is also suspect because it is not preserved in all of the manuscripts. In this episode, Odoric and some Franciscans from Peking are traveling along a road and encounter the Khan, who pays homage to the cross. This is not a real, proper conversion in the true sense of the word, but the Khan's reverence for the cross demonstrated, to the readers of the *Relatio,* the tremendous evangelistic potential of the eastern missions: the Khan seemed very ready to embrace the Word of God. It is difficult to say if this episode was part of Odoric's original account or, more likely, was a later addition serving other ends, such as the sending of other missionaries or the beatification of the monk. But it is certain that in the more widespread version of the text, this event crowns the voyage, showing its full success in that it meets the initial goal of saving souls. In this way, the circle of narration is complete.

The religious dimension in the *Relatio* is strongest in the long story that tells of the martyrdom of the four Franciscans of Tana, who were executed by Muslim authorities for their faith. The report may rely on a preexisting version of the event, which Odoric could have read in India or upon his return to Italy. It contains all the traditional characteristics of a hagiographic text. The brothers, arrested and accused of blaspheming Muhammad, firmly refused to retract their affirmations of faith; for this they underwent torture but came out unscathed, thanks to God's protection. They endured a long exposure to the scorching sun, beyond all human limits. James of Padua, who appears to have been their leader and spokesman, was burned at the stake but escaped unharmed. Their heroic behavior, and the obvious protection granted to them by God, made a great impression on the crowd, who were convinced of the friars' great faith and begged their persecutors to spare their lives. After death by the sword, their bodies displayed miraculous powers: they remained uncorrupted for a time; the bones, which Odoric carried with him to the Chinese Christian community, protected him during a fire; the same bones stirred up the wind so that he could continue on his journey by sea; even the dust of the site where the martyrdom took place manifested heal-

ing powers. The punishments that typically await the per-
petrators in classical accounts of martyrdom are not missing here: the *Melic* (or chief magistrate) of Tana was
executed by the emperor for his crime, and the *Cadi* (or religious leader) was forced into exile to escape the same
fate.

The religious dimension plays a much larger role in the
Relatio than in other travel accounts, partly because of the
disproportionate amount of space taken up by the martyrdom of the friars of Tana, but also because of Odoric's
many descriptions of the religious customs of the peoples
that he encountered on the way. It is clear, however, that he
considers most of these customs as bizarre or aberrant;
Odoric considered his religion unquestionably superior
and never demonstrated any tendency toward ecumenism
(which would in any case have been anachronistic for the
Middle Ages). He did observe certain rituals, though,
with particular interest and described them with vivacity.
He began with the naturalistic cults of southern Persia,
where they worshipped fire, trees, and snakes. He continued with the repugnant practices of the Malabar, where
idols, in the form of bovine creatures, demanded human
sacrifice and subjected their believers to the humiliation
of being sprinkled with excrement. He then went on to

describe the long, slow processions led by a gigantic Indian idol, during which many of the faithful threw themselves under the carriage wheels or, in a possessed, wild manner, committed ritual suicide. Then he moved on to the rites of cremation that occurred in the kingdom of Zampa, the effigies of the ox-god which the inhabitants of the islands of Nicoveran carried in front of them, and the great idols of Zayton to which sacrifices were made.

Sometimes, Odoric described the idolatrous ceremonies with horror, as just the beginning of an abyss of vileness. So it was that he told of the funerals that took place in Tibet, where a cadaver was dismembered and left in the open, to let the birds carry the remains to heaven; the son then took the head and ate the brain, keeping the skinned cranium to make a cup out of. Likewise, he recounts another anthropophagous practice on the island of Dondin, a place that cannot be precisely identified but that represents the culminating point of the primitive and exotic world of the Indian islands. ("In the whole world there be no such marvels as in that realm," Odoric said of India, immediately after having finished the blood-curdling description of Dondin.) In Dondin, an idol decided which sick people would live and which would die. If the idol said that the individual would be cured, the relatives would care for him according to the instructions received, and the sick person would apparently recover quickly. But if the idol declared that the illness was fatal, the unlucky individual would be killed by suffocation. His corpse would then be cut up and devoured by family members and other table companions. This time, Odoric discussed the matter with the natives, protesting the inhumanity of the ritual. But they declared that he was the inhuman one: they ate the body of the dead so that the worms would not be able to do it.

Only one other time did Odoric find himself involved in a religious dispute, at least in the broad sense; it was in Cansay, and the subject of the discussion was reincarnation. He was brought to a garden full of monkeys, which were attended to and revered by the monks. It was explained to him that those monkeys were the spirits of deceased nobility, reincarnated in noble animals. Odoric ridiculed this religious belief. But in this case, he seemed to emphasize, not the theological aspects, but the exoticism and oddness of this particular custom, which was shown to him in order to give him something extraordinary to report once he was back home again.

To tell the truth, Odoric had already seen a lot of unusual things, and the comparison of these things with the habits of the Europeans is continuous. He was especially struck by the differences in gender roles that he found. For example, in the land of Huz, the men, not the women, did the weaving; in Chaldea, he observed the women's clothing with much curiosity; in the region of Lamori (one of the most barbarous), the women, not the dwellings, were shared communally, to the point that when a child was born it was impossible, and not considered important, to determine the paternity; Chinese men were handsome, and Chinese women let their fingernails grow extremely long, both for ornament and to distinguish their social class.

Odoric frequently compares these new lands to the cities of northeast Italy, the region where he had previously lived and therefore knew well. Compared to Chinese cities, Treviso and Vicenza were just small villages; in contrast, the capital of Prester John's kingdom, which was widely believed to be so glorious, in fact was insignificant in comparison with Vicenza. The city of Censcalan was three times bigger than Venice and Zayton two times bigger than Bologna; some of the suburbs of Cansay, not to mention the main city itself, were as big as Venice and Padua; the floods of the Huang River reminded him of those that the river Po periodically inflicted on Ferrara; in certain zones of southern China, the normal population density was heavier than that found in Venice during the celebration of the Ascension.

It is interesting to note that in Odoric's accounts of the regions of India all is exotic and murky and there is a sense of constant danger, while China is described as well ordered, with everything in harmony in that noble and powerful civilization. For this reason, Lucio Monaco speaks of a spiritual itinerary beyond the material one: Odoric moves from the dark, disordered, and immoral Indian and Indo-Chinese regions to the luminous and well-ordered land of China, where the inhabitants seem close to conversion to Christ.

This interpretation may appear too schematic, and too many items in the text and in the modest literary quality of the work might keep us from thinking that such a plan was consciously followed. Odoric's admiration of China, however, is still undeniable — and indeed quite remarkable considering the fact that China was a non-Christian country. Certainly, we could not expect someone like Odoric to be as detached and impartial as an observer of today would be: in his view, he was travelling in pagan lands, among unsaved people who were prey to the devil. But Odoric showed remarkable openness and objectivity for his day. He demonstrated a liking for the people that he met and showed an involvement and interest in their culture and sentiments. Conversion was his objective, but he was capable of seeing many aspects of these peoples as both positive and original. This was still the Middle Ages, when being Christian was an essential characteristic of being European, but yet a period without the fundamentalisms and the fears that would arise later, when evangelism was done by means of guns and swords. One of the more unique and modern aspects of Odoric's account lies in his respect for diversity.

A voyager's curiosity and the pleasure he took in noting the bizarre or the incredible often prevailed over the strictly religious component, which was the basis of his travels. From the beginning, the reader is struck by this aspect of the *Relatio,* with the story of the man who tamed the partridges and took them around with him as he pleased, a story recounted with spontaneity and an enjoyment of narration for narration's sake. This story is not a type of *exemplum;* no type of symbolic analogy is underlined, and one cannot find a trace of moral preaching. Facts are simply collected and retold. The *Relatio* thus unfolds a series of facts, objects, various phenomena, plants, animals, and people, each unusual in some way. Along the road, one after the other, Odoric comes upon mountains of salt, impenetrable deserts, crocodiles, mice as big as dogs, men with extremely long testicles, trees that produce bread, fantastic palaces, magic fish, snakes, elephants, leeches, bamboo reeds, precious stones of amazing size and luminosity, sensational pearls, gigantic tortoises, birds of unusual appearances, men with the head of a dog, hens covered in wool, lambs born of melons, and women equipped with fangs. At various times, in the course of the *Relatio*, Odoric realizes how difficult it must be to believe what he is telling the reader and says that he would not have believed it himself, if he had not seen it.

Geographers and ethnographers alike have tried to identify the objects and events described by Odoric, and they tend to believe that the account is substantially credible, notwithstanding the inevitable exaggerations and additions that creep into an oral report given from memory. The least convincing parts of the narration concern things that Odoric heard from others but did not see himself. His account of the extraordinary island of Dondin — an unidentified place where everything was primitive, bestial, and grotesque — appears to be more an imaginative addition or exaggeration than something real. Even in this case, however, the narration most likely has some basis in real events that Odoric himself observed or heard of while on the islands of the Indian Ocean or the Sonda Islands. The episode of the infernal valley is the last story that can be shown to have been part of the original draft of the work; because the narration contains obvious exaggerations, it is difficult to ferret out the real facts. But such exaggeration pertains to only a few cases — limited, in fact, to a small number of episodes in which some religious or moral preaching creeps in. In these few cases, Odoric becomes more a preacher or teacher than a narrator or curious traveller. Perhaps in these cases Odoric is more medieval: in these rare episodes, the accent is no longer on the veracity of what is told but on the function of the account, on its usefulness in demonstrating and teaching moral truths.

There can be no doubt, however, that the account is substantially truthful; today, all the exegetes acknowledge that what is written in the *Relatio* has a basis in reality, despite the skepticism of the past. Such criticism came mainly from the fact that Odoric's original manuscript was confused with the later fictional rewriting done by Sir John Mandeville. The pieces of the *Relatio* that can best be verified are those which can be compared with outside sources, for which Odoric's account often provides clarification and added details. For example, the most detailed part of the work — which describes the court of the Great Khan's palace in Cambalech, the ceremonies at court, the imperial pastimes and hunts, and the communications system — is all undoubtedly the fruit of direct and documented observation on the part of our traveller. Odoric proved himself diligent in distinguishing between observations he made firsthand and accounts that he received from others. He was ready to express skepticism when something seemed doubtful; concerning the lake on the island of Sri Lanka, Odoric clearly stated that, although the natives believed it to have been formed from the tears of Adam and Eve, this amounted to pure fantasy because the lake was really fed by underground springs.

It has been noted that Odoric often observed the same things that Marco Polo had observed and reported some decades before him; one can suspect, in some cases at least, a dependence on this source and, as a result, information that is less authentic. We cannot know if Odoric had actually read Polo's work, but it is probable that he knew of it; after all, the two writers lived in the same area, and it would be natural that, before departing, our traveller would want to know what awaited him, or, once back home in Italy, that he would want to compare his experiences with those of his famous predecessor. Though we cannot be certain that Odoric knew of this literary work, *Livre des marveilles du monde,* we can be sure that the information that he brought from the East became part of an already-acquired body of knowledge, circulating at least orally if not also in written form. Fantastic stories of the Orient must have been spreading in Venice and Padua, brought there by Marco Polo and others; and Odoric's account would have been compared with these other reports. Therefore, it is inevitable that Odoric's listeners and readers asked for information on the things they were expecting to hear about. From such interactions between Odoric and his audience the *Relatio* would have been born. Thus it should not surprise us that the episode of the Old Man of the Mountain resembles Marco Polo's account a little too closely, nor should Odoric's account be valued any less because it is not completely original. Simply stated, the writer(s) of the *Relatio* (Odoric, or maybe even more than he, other Franciscans of Padua who attended to the rewriting of the report) could not but ponder on this episode, because the public already knew about it and wanted to hear more about it.

The interaction with the public was also probably responsible for the more strictly mercantile notations of the

Relatio, which might seem foreign to the mentality of a Franciscan friar so dedicated to his missionary work. It can be justified, though, if we think of his readers, for whom the East was not just a wonderful land but also a real or potential source of wealth. On every leg of his trip, Odoric records the riches of the zone in question, the typical products, the climatic features, and the fertility of the soil; it is clear that this is not merely a matter of simple curiosity but instead concerns commercial possibilities, because he generally cites those products that could be obtained very cheaply. Many times, he even quotes the Venetian wholesale cost of these goods. Thus we discover that in Tauris salt cost next to nothing, that Iest was the best place for figs and raisins, and that partridges could be bought very cheaply in the land of Huz. Of greater interest is the fact that pepper was found on the coast of Malabar, that ginger could be bought very inexpensively in Censcalan, and that sugar was cheap in Zayton. Sunzumayu was the best place to buy silk, and rhubarb was available in the internal region of Shaanxi. For each region, Odoric also gives information concerning personal property, the use of currency, and units of account and measurement. This is a far cry from a merchant's manual, which Odoric certainly did not intend to write; nevertheless, it is clear that the *Relatio* could not leave out of consideration the cultural and geographic context in which it was written, nor the expectations of its audience, nor the foreknowledge of its compilers and readers. We have, therefore, a work that presents multiple aspects and diverse dimensions due to a special interaction between a religious author and a prevalently lay audience, which had centuries-old models and expectations.

It must be acknowledged that the literary level of the *Relatio* is rather modest. The work shows only slight hints of the good rhetorical and stylistic education that could be obtained in the religious or town schools of northern Italy. Whoever compiled it knew enough Latin to be able to write it, but certainly not enough to compose a refined book. Subsequent copyists and lectors strove to adjust the form of the work, correcting the main grammatical and syntactical errors and arranging the sentences in a way that would be more engaging to its audience. The Italian colloquialisms are overdone, in some parts being favored over the corresponding Latin phrases. Except for a pair of Bible quotations (predictable and really inevitable in this context), quotes from other works are all but absent, whereas in other medieval writings they are generally very frequent. The few references to history or even to religious history that are found in the *Relatio* appear, on the one hand, very suspect (they are not found in all of the manuscripts, and therefore their authenticity is not certain) and, on the other hand, rather banal. Furthermore, in all of the *Relatio,* not a single book is mentioned as having been read or even seen by anyone. At the court of the Great Khan, we hear of dishes and utensils, games and jugglers, precious stones and gold leaf — but not a single book. Paper is referred only with regard to making money from it. Simply stated, it can be said that for Odoric books were not important. Odoric's culture and learning must have been modest, not much higher than that of the average Franciscan friars of that time. All in all, the image that we can form of his personality does not fit that of a scholar. If anything, he is the prototype of the militant Franciscan, poor by choice, who, having renounced the world, also renounces scholastic refinement in order to dedicate himself totally to the work of evangelization for Christ.

The *Relatio* of Odoric of Pordenone met with considerable success in Europe in the Low Middle Ages. Various manuscripts of Odoric's travel account, written in Latin, circulated in Europe beginning in the years immediately following his death. The account was translated twice in French, once in German, and at least seven times in Italian. Following paths not always easy to establish, but probably tied to existing connections between diverse Franciscan monasteries, the text came to be read from Spain to Poland and from southern Italy to England. It was most widespread, however, in Odoric's home region, the territories of Veneto and Friuli, where he died in the odor of sanctity and where important Franciscan monasteries were found, especially the one in Padua. The *Relatio* also circulated widely in the Austrian and Bohemian regions, where it was introduced by Henry of Glarus, who, as previously stated, had known Odoric in Avignon. In England, a special edition of the text was fairly common in the 1400s, one that bore the signature of the notary Guecello and that must have originally included a list of Odoric's miracles. It is this copy of the work that has preserved for us the legend of the miraculous prediction to Odoric of his death.

As already noted, Odoric's *Relatio* does not seem to be a completely authentic text. Its origin goes back to the stories that he told his brethren, once he had returned to Italy, and these could have been transcribed several times and in various ways. In addition to the most widespread form of the text there are, in fact, other compilations in Latin and in Italian that are sometimes very dissimilar;

these compilations include episodes and information that are not found in the vulgate version, but that, because of certain features, could possibly be authentic. Apparently the oldest account ended with the story of Odoric's visit to the infernal valley (chapter 49), and many manuscripts of the work break off at that point. Later, the important story that tells of the Great Khan paying homage to the cross (chapter 51) was added, in a position that is incongruous from a geographic point of view. According to some manuscripts (including those followed in the translation presented here), we owe the recollection of this episode to Brother Marchesino of Bassano, who lived in the Franciscan monastery of Padua. In Henry of Glarus's edition, the report of the Khan's reverence to the cross is given in an appendix separate from the text. The most widespread version of the *Relatio,* however, bears the signature of another Paduan monk, William of Solagna. In this edition, the story of the Khan and the cross is incorporated into the narration and Marchesino's name is not cited. In certain manuscripts of William's compilation, the stories of the miracles attributed to Odoric after his death were added in a way that created a dossier, the aim of which was clearly to further his beatification. In still other manuscripts of the Italian and Latin versions, vari-

ous other episodes are found, as already noted, which may
or may not have been genuine.

In later years, many copyists and lectors did not hesi-
tate to modify the text in various ways, sometimes adding
details taken from other sources, sometimes correcting the
rather rough linguistic form, and at still other times
changing various details tied to Odoric's context in a small
region of Italy. In one edition of the text that circulated in
southern Germany, identified several years ago by Folker
Reichert, the frequent comparisons that the *Relatio* makes
between Chinese cities and Italian ones were modified to
refer instead to German cities. Similar changes were made
in a Latin version of the text, preserved in only one manuscript that is kept today in Milan; this version had obviously been drawn up in France because the comparisons
are made to French cities and rivers. Because Odoric of
Pordenone was almost unknown outside the small Franciscan sphere of Veneto and Friuli, his name did not carry
enough authority to safeguard the integrity of his work, as
would have been the case if the author had been more famous and prestigious. In addition, the simple literary
quality of the work, its discursive and almost oral style,
and its rich use of Italian colloquialisms all permitted
copyists and lectors over the years to change it in ways

more akin to the grammatical and literary tastes of their own epoch. All of this, plus the vast quantity of manuscripts of the work, makes it even more difficult to reconstruct the original version of the *Relatio* accurately. A comprehensive study of the entire history of the complete set of manuscripts has yet to be done, even though individual analyses of the various editions of the text allow us today to have a much clearer picture of the situation.

We have chosen here to re-present the English translation that Sir Henry Yule gave in his volume *Cathay and the Way Thither*, published by the Hakluyt Society in 1866. It is a translation of great historical value, thanks also to the personality and the competence of the author. Henry Yule (1820-1889) lived in India for more than twenty years, serving in the British army. He earned the rank of colonel and was given meritorious mention for his involvement in expanding the irrigation works of the area and developing the railroad network. From his father, who was a high official in the India Company, he inherited a library rich in Arabic and Persian texts. Above all, the father instilled in his son a passion for literature and ethnography, which Henry cultivated and broadened during his sojourn in India. In 1862, Henry returned to Europe, establishing himself in Palermo, Sicily, where he was able to continue his studies undisturbed. In the following years, he published three works that he had conceived and drafted while still in India and had revised in Italy: *Mirabilia descripta: The Wonders of the East* (1863), *Cathay and the Way Thither* (1866), and an edition of Marco Polo's *Livre des merveilles du monde* (1871). Of the three, the latter work had the greatest success, partly because of the popularity of the topic; reprinted in 1875, it won awards from the Italian Geographic Society and the Royal Geographical Society. In 1875, he went back to England, where he resided until his death, never giving up his studies (he was also president of the Hakluyt Society) and continuing to involve himself in the political life of colonial India.

Cathay and the Way Thither consists of two volumes, comprised of seven monographic essays that touch on the various texts, episodes, and features of European explorations and missions to the East between the late Middle Ages and modern times. In the long introduction to the first volume, which takes up more than two hundred and fifty pages, Yule outlines a history of the relations between China and Europe, from antiquity to the Mongol period. His work is furnished with an exhaustive anthology of noteworthy items about the Far East that were found in the works of geographers of ancient and medieval times. The second essay is dedicated to Odoric and includes historical-biographic information and the English translation of the *Relatio*, supplied with a vast array of explanatory notes. The successive essays are dedicated, respectively, to the letters sent to the West by the missionaries of the 1300s; the travel accounts of the Arab physician Rashiduddin (who lived for a long time at the Mongolian court); the commercial manual of the Florentine merchant Francesco Balducci Pegolotti (about 1340); the writings of John of Marignola; the reports on the Far East written by the Arab geographer Ibn Battuda (1347); and finally, the journey to China made by the Portuguese Benedict Goes (seventeenth century). In the appendix, Yule also included two compilations of Odoric's *Relatio*, one in Latin, the other in Italian, and added a rich and important critical summary. In spite of its age, Yule's work continues to constitute a fundamental study for many of the subjects discussed and does not cease to amaze its readers because of the wealth of information it offers and its competent critical analysis.

We have already noted that many versions of the *Relatio* are preserved today, yet Odoric's original account is still far from being accurately reconstructed. Among the various manuscripts of the work, Yule utilized a codex in the

National Library of Paris (lat. 2584) as the base text, integrating other information that he found in other manuscripts (especially the Latin manuscripts XIV.43 and the Italian ones VI.102, in the Marciana Library in Venice, and manuscript E.5.9.6-7 in the National Library of Florence). The advantages and the limits of this choice were very clear to Yule, who wrote regarding his translation:

It will be obvious that before preparing a translation, it becomes necessary (on the principle of catching your hare before cooking it) to ascertain the text which is to be translated. The determination *verbatim* of a standard text is not possible under the circumstances, but fortunately a large proportion of the variations disappear in translation, as they are not variations in sense. As regards the variations in proper names, in most cases it is possible to deduce from the facts which reading is nearest to the truth, though often considerable study has been necessary to ascertain their real indications. Among the variations in other matters, the editor has exercised his judgement in selecting what seemed to be the most probable readings. And where it seemed a pity to omit additional particulars that were curious or interesting, though depending on doubtful or exceptional authority, these have been interpolated into the translation within brackets.

Yule's methodical approach, even today, appears to be rational and acceptable, and his beautiful translation provides us with a precise and fascinating idea of Odoric's text. Philological critique and historical investigation have made notable progress with respect to that period, and other manuscripts today are considered superior to those Yule utilized. But still today, as then, it is not possible to determine or reconstruct Odoric's "original" text in an unambiguous fashion. This might become possible in the future, but only after an extensive examination of its entire written tradition and after critical research to comprehend better the text's stratifications and to eliminate those elements of Odoric's work which were added at a later date. For the moment, Yule's translation, because of its historic value and its literary importance, remains unsurpassed.

The comments in the footnotes aim at helping the reader to understand correctly the text of the *Relatio.* Whenever possible, they help to identify the principal places Odoric spoke about or travelled through. They are purely orientational comments because the scope of the present publication is to provide the English public with an opportunity to appreciate the text for what it is: a travel account and a literary work. These comments are indebted, to a major extent, to the ample notes of Yule,

Cordier, and Pullé, which still remain the basis of the text's exegesis. When possible, the facts have been updated on the basis of more recent research. For the transcription of the names of Chinese cities, and Asian cities in general, *The Times Atlas of the World* was used, as well as the Chinese cartography of Chiao-Min Hsieh and Jean Kan Hsieh (*China: A Provincial Atlas* [New York, 1995]).

Bibliography

Cathay and the Way Thither was published in London in 1866 by the Hakluyt Society; a second edition, revised and expanded by Henry Cordier, was published in 1913 by the Hakluyt Society, again with the same title.

Before and after Yule's edition, the Latin text of the *Relatio* was the subject of other versions, mostly from single manuscripts. The most important of these were the following: R. Hakluyt, *The Second Volume of the Principal Navigations, Voyages, Traffiques and Discoveries* (London, 1599), pp. 39-53; *Acta Sanctorum Ianuarii* I (Antwerp, 1643), pp. 268-74; G. Venni, *Elogio storico alle gesta del Beato Odorico* (Venice, 1761), pp. 46-83; K. E. Aurivillius, *Itinerarium Odorici Forojuliensis Ordinis Minorum* (Uppsala, 1817); Marcellino di

Civezza, *Storia universale delle missioni francescane* III (Rome, 1859), pp. 741-81; T. Domenichelli, *Sopra la vita e i viaggi del Beato Odorico da Pordenone dell'Ordine dei Minori* (Prato, 1881) [anastatic reprinting: Odoric of Pordenone, *Relazione del viaggio in Oriente e in Cina (1314?-1330)* (Pordenone, 1982), pp. 73-120]; A. Van den Wyngaert, *Sinica Franciscana* I (Florence-Quaracchi, 1929), pp. 413-95 (at the moment this is the current reference edition for the Latin text); A. Sartori, "Odoriciana, Vita e memorie," *Il Santo* 6 (1966): 36-65; R. K. Carlson, *Odoric of Pordenone — Traveller to the Far East: A Restoration of a Recently Discovered Manuscript of Odoric's Journal* (Ph.D. diss., University of Kansas, 1977).

The majority of the Italian, French, and German versions have also been published: G. B. Ramusio, *Navigationi et viaggi* II (Venice, 1574); H. Cordier, *Les voyages en Asie au XIV siècle du bienheureux Frère Odoric de Pordenone, réligieux de Saint-François* (Paris, 1891); G. Strasmann, *Konrad Steckels deutsche Übertragung der Reise nach China des Odorico de Pordenone* (Berlin, 1968); Odoric of Pordenone, *Memoriale toscano. Viaggio in India e Cina (1318-1330),* edited by L. Monaco (Alexandria, 1990); Jean de Vignay, *Les merveilles de la Terre d'Outremer,* edited by D. A. Trotter (Exeter, 1990).

Specific studies of the text of the *Relatio,* in addition to the introductions to the various editions, are those of

C. Petrocchi, "Il beato Odorico da Pordenone e il suo 'Itinerario'," *Le Venezie francescane* 2 (1933): 71-84; L. Monaco, "I volgarizzamenti italiani della relazione di Odorico da Pordenone," *Studi mediolatini e volgari* 26 (1978-79): 179-220; G. C. Testa, "Bozza per un censimentco dei manoscritti odoriciani," in *Odorico da Pordenone e la Cina. Atti del convegno storico internazionale, Pordenone, 28-29 maggio 1982* (Pordenone, 1983), pp. 117-50; F. Reichert, "Eine unbekannte Version der Asienreise Odorichs von Pordenone," *Deutsches Archiv für Erforschung des Mittelalters* 62 (1987): 531-73; A. Andreose, "'Lo libro dele nove e stranie meravioxe cose', Ricerche sui volgarizzamenti italiani dell' 'Itinerarium' del beato Odorico da Pordenone," *Il Santo* 38 (1998): 31-67; P. Chiesa, "Per un riordino della tradizione manoscritta della *Relatio* di Odorico da Pordenone," *Fliologia Mediolatina* 6-7 (1999-2000): 311-50.

Concerning Odoric's personality, his life, and his journeys see the following: *Chronica XXIV Generalium Ordinis Minorum,* Analecta Franciscana, III (Florence-Quaracchi, 1897), pp. 499-504; G. Golubovich, "II b. fr. Odorico da Pordenone O.F.M. Note critiche bio-bibliografiche," *Archivum Franciscanum Historicum* 10 (1917): 17-46; A. C. Moule, "A Small Contribution in the Study of the Bibliography of Odoric," *T'oung Pao* 20 (1921): 301-22; G. Pullé,

Viaggio del Beato Odorico di Pordenone (Milan, 1931); C. Schmitt, "Il Beato Odorico da Pordenone: appunti bibliografici," in *Odorico da Pordenone e la Cina. Atti del convegno storico internazionale, Pordenone, 28-29 maggio 1982* (Pordenone, 1983), pp. 151-62.

For information about western travellers in the Far East in the fourteenth century and their accounts see M. Komroff, *Contemporaries of Marco Polo, Consisting of the Travel Records to the Eastern Parts in the World* (London, 1929); L. Olschki, *L'Asia di Marco Polo* (Venice-Rome, 1957); Chr. Dawson, *Mission to Asia: Narratives and Letters of the Franciscan Missionaries in Mongolia and China in the Thirteenth and Fourteenth Centuries* (New York, 1966, orig. 1955); P. Pelliot, *Recherches sur les chrétiens d'Asie Centrale et d'Extrême Orient* (Paris, 1973); A. C. Moule, *Christians in China before the Year 1550* (New York, 1977); L. Petech, "I francescani nell'Asia centrale e orientale nel XIII e XIV secolo," in *Espansione del francescanesimo fra Occidente e Oriente nel secolo XIII* (Assisi, 1979), pp. 213-40; J. Richard, *Croisés, missionaires et voyageurs. Les perspectives orientales du monde latin médiéval* (London, 1983); Giovanni di Pian del Carpine, *Storia dei Mongoli,* edited by E. Menestò, M. C. Lungarotti, P. Daffinà, L. Petech, and C. Leopardi (Spoleto, 1989); F. Reichert, *Begegnungen mit China. Die Entdeckungen Ostasiens im Mittelalter* (Sigmaringen,

1992); E. Menestò, "Relazioni di viaggi e ambasciatori," in *Lo spazio letterario del Medioevo* I: *Il medioevo latino*, 1, 2 (Rome, 1993), pp. 535-600.

THE EASTERN PARTS OF
THE WORLD DESCRIBED

*by Friar Odoric the Bohemian, of Friuli,
in the Province of Saint Anthony.*

1. What the Friar saw at Trebizond
and in the Greater Armenia.

Albeit many other stories of sundry kinds concerning the customs and peculiarities of different parts of this world have been related by a variety of persons, yet would I have you to know that I also, Friar Odoric of Friuli,[1] can truly rehearse many great marvels which I did hear and see when, according to my wish, I crossed the sea and vis-

---

1. In the manuscripts, Odoric's homeland is sometimes given as Friuli, that is, the name of the region, and at other times as Pordenone, the name of the city.

ited the countries of the unbelievers in order to win some harvest of souls [and this I did with the leave of my superiors, who have power to grant it by the rules of our Order].[2]

[Wherefore I purpose to relate briefly and compendiously under sundry chapters of this little work a multitude of the things which I have seen and heard in the East and the North and the South. Of all I purpose not to speak, though I shall be the first to tell of many which will seem to a number of people past belief. Nor, indeed, could I myself have believed these things, had I not heard them with my own ears or seen the like myself. Fourteen years and a half, in the habit of Francis, that blessed confessor of Christ, I sojourned in those parts of the world. And now being at Padua, I have here compiled this little work at the request of the reverend Friar Guidotto, the minister of the province of Saint Anthony. If, then, the studious reader shall find anything good in it, let him ascribe that to the divine bounty and not to my poor skill.

2. This clarification is found in the version of the text edited by Henry of Glarus, and certainly derives from a preoccupation with portraying the pattern of Odoric's journey as less anarchic, seeing that it was not born of an official initiative.

And if he find anything too hard for belief, and wherein he judgeth me to stray from truth, let him remark thereon with a student's charity, and not with insolent bitterness and spiteful snarling.]3

First, then, [going with the galleys from Venice] I crossed over the Greater Sea, and so passed to Trebizond,4 which was of old called Pontus. This city is situated passing well, and is a haven for the Persians, Medes, and all the people on the further side of the sea. And in this country I saw a very pretty sight [which I am the more bold to tell, because many persons with whom I have spoken in Venice assure me that they have seen the like]. I beheld a certain man taking about with him more than four thousand partridges. For as the man went along the ground, the partridges followed him flying in the air. These partridges he was then taking to a certain castle which is called Zegana,

3. This long paragraph gives the reader, among other things, an idea of the length of the voyage. It is found in a group of four Latin manuscripts that give evidence of the edition of the *Relatio* which includes, in the final part, the story of the Great Khan's homage to the cross, as it was recounted by Odoric to Brother Marchesino of Bassano.

4. Today Trabzon, on the northern coast of Anatolia; in the Low Middle Ages it was the seat of the so-called empire of Trebizond, controlled for a long time by the Byzantine Comnenus dynasty.

distant three days' journey from Trebizond,[5] [where they dig copper and crystal]. And the way with these partridges was this, that whenever the man wanted to lie down or go to sleep, they all gathered about him like chickens about a hen. And in this manner he took them along to Trebizond, to the palace of the emperor; and he, when they were thus brought before him, took as many partridges as he desired; but the rest of them the man led back to the place whence he had first brought them.

In this same city (of Trebizond) is deposited the body of Athanasius,[6] over one of the gates of the city; of him, that is, that made the creed which beginneth *Quicumque vult salvus esse* ("whoever wants to be saved"). Departing thence, I came into Armenia the Greater, to a certain city which is called Arziron, which in time long past was a fine and most wealthy city, and it would have been so unto this day but for the Tartars and the Saracens who have done it

5. Three days' march, southward from Trabzon, along the caravan road to Erzurum.

6. Athanasius, to whom the creed cited in this passage is attributed (erroneously), was the famous patriarch of Alexandria, who lived in the fourth century. It has not been proven, though, that his remains were ever preserved in Trebizond. He is probably confused here with a local saint of the same name.

much damage. It aboundeth greatly in bread and flesh, and many other kinds of victual, but not in wine or fruits. For the city is mighty cold, and folk say that it is the highest city that is at this day inhabited on the whole face of the earth.[7] But it hath most excellent water, the reason whereof seems to be that the springs of this water are derived from the river Euphrates, which floweth at about one day's journey from the city. And this city is just midway to Tauris.

Departing from it, I came to a certain hill which is called Sarbisacalo;[8] and in that country is the mountain whereon is Noah's Ark. And I would fain have ascended it, if my companions would have waited for me. But the folk of the country told us that no one ever could ascend the

7. Erzurum is situated at an altitude of about two thousand meters in the eastern extremity of the Anatolian plateau.

8. Mount Sarbisacalo (which, in the manuscripts, also appears with the spelling of Solissaculo or Sobissacalo) has never been identified with precision. According to Yule, it could refer to a peak located twenty-four miles southeast of Erzurum. Noah's Ark, according to tradition, was discovered on Mount Ararat, the imposing massif in Armenia, over five thousand meters high, which rises to the north of the caravan route that connected Erzurum to Tabriz, near the modern city of Dogubayazit.

mountain, for this, as it is said, hath seemed not to be the pleasure of the Most High.

2. Concerning the city of Tauris and the city of Soldania, where dwelleth the Persian Emperor.

From that country I passed to Tauris,[9] a great city and a royal, which anciently was called Susis,[10] and was the city of the King Ahasuerus. In it they say the Arbor Secco[11] existeth in a mosque, that is to say, in a church of the Saracens. And this is a nobler city and a better for merchandise than any other which at this day existeth in the world.

9. Today's Tabriz, regional capital of Iranian Azerbaijan.

10. The identification of Tabriz with Susa, one of the metropolises of the ancient Persian Empire, was common in the Middle Ages, but mistaken. Susa was actually located on the border between Iran and Mesopotamia, not far from the modern city of Dezful.

11. The "Dry Tree." Ruy Comiez of Clavijo also speaks of this tree, in the account of the embassy that travelled to Tamerlane, on behalf of the king of Castile, at the beginning of the fifteenth century. The legend that Clavijo recounts tells of a tree that will flower on the day in which a Christian bishop, at the head of a crowd of faithful, arrives in the city with the intention of evangelizing the region.

For there is not on the face of the earth any kind of provision, or any species of goods, but you will find great store thereof at Tauris. It is admirable for situation, and so opulent a city that you would scarcely believe the things to be found there; for the whole world, almost, hath dealings with that city for merchandise. And the Christians will tell you that the emperor there hath more revenue from that one city than the king of France hath from his whole realm. Near that city is a mountain of salt, which furnisheth great store of salt for the whole place. And of this salt taketh every man as much as he listeth, and payeth nothing to any man. In that city, also, there dwell many Christians of every description, but the Saracens have the rule over them in all things. And there are many things else to be said of that city, but it would take too long to relate them.

Departing from this city of Tauris, I travelled for ten days, and reached a certain city called Soldania,[12] in which dwelleth the emperor of the Persians in the summer sea-

12. Today Soltaniyeh is a spot of modest importance southeast of Zanjan. In the Middle Ages it was one of the principal cities of the region, the site of a flourishing Franciscan community and, later, of a Catholic bishopric.

son. But in the winter he goeth to a certain other place [called Axam] which is on the sea called the Sea of Bacuc.[13] This city (of Soldania) is a great one, and a cool place, with an excellent supply of water, and many costly wares are brought thither for sale.

3. Concerning the city of the Magi; also of the Sea of Sand, and of the land of Huz.

Departing from this city with a caravan, that is to say with a certain company, I proceeded in the direction of Upper India, and after travelling that way for many days I halted at the city of the three Magi, which is called Cassan,[14] a royal city and of great repute. But the Tartars have greatly destroyed it. It is a city which aboundeth greatly in bread and wine, and in many other good things. From this city to Jerusalem (whither the Magi found their way, not surely

13. The Caspian Sea; the name "Sea of Bacuc" derived from the city of Baku, then, as now, the main port on the western shore.

14. Today's Kashan, approximately two hundred kilometers south of Teheran. The home city of the Magi, which the New Testament generically placed in the Orient, was identified in various ways in the Middle Ages, but only Odoric placed it as Kashan.

by human strength but by Divine strength working by miracle, seeing how quickly they went), is a good fifty days' journey. And there be many other things with regard to that city which it boots not much to rehearse.

Passing thence I travelled to a certain city called Iest[15] [which is the furthest city of Persia towards India], from which the Sea of Sand is but one day distant. Now that sea is a wondrous thing, and right perilous. [And there were none of us who desired to enter on that sea. For it is all of dry sand without the slightest moisture. And it shifteth as the sea doth when in storm, now hither, now thither, and as it shifteth it maketh waves in like manner as the sea doth; so that countless people travelling thereon have been overwhelmed and drowned and buried in those sands. For when blown about and buffeted by the winds, they are raised into hills, now in this place, now in that, according as the wind chanceth to blow.] In this city of Iest there is very great store of victuals and all other good things that you can mention; but especially is found there great plenty of figs; and raisins also, green as grass and very small, are found there in richer profusion than in any

15. Modern Yazd, about five hundred kilometers southeast of Teheran.

other part of the world. This is the third best city which the emperor of the Persians possesses in his whole realm. The Saracens say of it that no Christian is ever able to live in it beyond one year. And there are many other matters there.

Departing thence, and passing by many cities and towns, I came to a certain city by the name of Comerum,[16] which formerly was a great city, and in the olden time did great scathe to the Romans. The compass of its walls is a good fifty miles, and there be therein palaces yet standing entire, but without inhabitants. It aboundeth, however, in many kinds of victual.

Leaving this and going on through many towns and cities I reached the city called Huz,[17] which abounds in all

16. This locality has not been placed with accuracy. If the mention of its past splendor refers to the Persian city of Persepolis, which is possible, it could be speaking of the area of Kenareh, northeast of Shiraz.

17. Concerning the identification of the place where the biblical Job lived, there has been much discussion from the time of the first exegesis. It is not even clear to which land Odoric was referring, because the last geographic indication that he gives ("this land adjoineth the extremity of Chaldea towards the North") would lead us to move the location to modern Syria. But this seems contradictory to the itinerary

kinds of victuals, and is beautifully situated. For near this city are mountains, which afford in great abundance the finest of pastures for cattle. There also is found manna of better quality and in greater abundance than in any part of the world. In that country also you can get four good partridges for less than a Venetian groat. In those parts also you see very comely elders; and 'tis the custom there for the men to knit and spin, and not the women. And this land adjoineth the extremity of Chaldea towards the North.

---

that Odoric had followed up to that point. Another hypothesis, at first sustained by Yule, would place it as Khuzestan, the low Mesopotamian plain, near the mouths of the Tigris and Euphrates Rivers. At any rate, the passage that Odoric took from the lands of Huz and Chaldea, described in the following chapter, signifies a digression with respect to the more direct route to India. Provided that the recollections of the traveller are not in some way confused, we must suppose that he stopped for some time in Persia, and, from there, made a trip west, re-tracing his steps later.

4. Fr. Odoric treateth of the manners of the people of Chaldea; of India within land; and of Ormes.

Departing thence I went into Chaldea,[18] which is a great kingdom, and as I went thither I passed by the Tower of Babel, which is distant perchance four days' journey from (the city). And in this land of Chaldea they have a language of their own; and the men are comely, but the women in sooth of an ill favor. The men indeed go smartly dressed and decked as our women go here, and on their heads they wear a kind of fillet of gold and pearls; whilst the women have nothing on them but a miserable shift reaching to the knees, and with sleeves so long and wide that they sweep the ground. And they go barefoot with drawers hanging about their feet, and their hair neither plaited nor braided, but in complete dishevelment; and as here among us the men go first and the women follow, so there the women have to go before the men. [Here I saw a young man who was taking to wife a beautiful young woman, and she was

18. The Chaldea of which Odoric speaks would seem to be identifiable with modern Iraq, as was commonly done in the Middle Ages, and particularly with the territory of Baghdad. It would seem so from the mention of the Tower of Babel, whose presumed ruins were shown a hundred or so kilometers from the city.

accompanied by other beautiful maidens, who were weeping and wailing, whilst the young bridegroom stood by in very gay clothes, with his head hanging down. And by and by the young man mounted his ass, and the bride followed him barefoot and wretchedly dressed, and holding by the ass, and her father went behind blessing them until they reached the husband's house.] And many other matters there be in this city which it booteth not greatly to detail.

So going thence I came to inland India,[19] a region which the Tartars have greatly wasted. And there you find people who live almost entirely on dates, and you get forty-two pounds of dates for less than a groat; and so of many other things.

Quitting this India and traversing many places, I came to the Ocean Sea. And the first city on it that I reached is called Ormes,[20] a city strongly fenced and abounding in costly wares. [The city is on an island some five miles distant from the main ; and on it there grows no tree, and there is no fresh water. There is indeed great plenty of

19. The "inland India" that Odoric speaks about corresponds to the southern coast of Iran, which faces the Persian Gulf and the Gulf of Oman.

20. The city of Hormuz, today's Bandar-Abbas, the main port on the strait that links the Persian Gulf to the Indian Ocean.

bread and fish and flesh. But it is not a healthy place nor safe for life, and the heat is something incredible. The people both men and women are all very tall. And where I passed by one day there was one just dead; and they had got together all the players in the place, and they set the dead man on his bed in the middle of the house, whilst two women danced round about him, and the players played on their cymbals and other instruments of music. Then two of the women took hold of the dead man, embracing him and chanting his praises, and the other women stood up one after another and took a pipe and piped on it awhile, and when one had done piping she sat down; and so they went on all night. And in the morning they carried him to the tomb.]21

5. Of ships that have no iron in their frame; and in such an one Fr. Odoric passeth to Tana in India.

In this country men make use of a kind of vessel which they call *Jase,* which is fastened only with stitching of twine.

21. This description of the usages and customs of Hormuz does not appear in the majority of the manuscripts of the *Relatio.*

On one of these vessels I embarked, and I could find no iron at all therein. And having thus embarked, I passed over in twenty-eight days to Tana,[22] where for the faith of Christ four of our Minor Friars had suffered a glorious martyrdom. The city is excellent in position, and hath great store of bread and wine, and aboundeth in trees. This was a great place in days of old, for it was the city of King Porus, who waged so great a battle with King Alexander.[23] The people thereof are idolaters, for they worship fire, and serpents, and trees also. The land is under the dominion of the Saracens, who have taken it by force of arms, and they are now subject to the empire of Dili.[24]

Here be found sundry kinds of beasts, and especially black lions in very great numbers, besides monkeys and baboons, and bats as big as pigeons are here. There be also

22. A city on the island of Salsetta, near modern Bombay.

23. The stories of Alexander the Great's expedition into India are often romanticized and have been widespread since the Hellenistic Age; they were also very popular in the Middle Ages. The story of the war between the Macedonian king and Porus, the king of India, is among these; it tells of Porus's heading into battle at the head of a herd of elephants, but of his being defeated all the same.

24. It would be, as Yule supposed, the empire of Delhi, namely, the Indian Empire.

rats as big as are our dogs called *scherpi*.[25] And for this reason rats are there caught by dogs, for the mousers or cats
are of no use for that. In this country every man hath before his house a plant of twigs as thick as a pillar would be
here, and this never withers as long as it gets water.[26] And
many other strange things are there which it would be
pretty to hear tell.

[The women go naked there, and when a woman is
married she is set on a horse, and the husband gets on the
crupper and holds a knife pointed at her throat; and they
have nothing on except a high cap on their head like a
mitre, wrought with white flowers, and all the maidens of
the place go singing in a row in front of them till they
reach the house, and there the bride and bridegroom are
left alone, and when they get up in the morning they go
naked as before.]

[In this country there are trees which give wine which
they call *loahc,* and which is very intoxicating. And here they
do not bury the dead, but carry them with great pomp to

25. These animals have not been identified; various manuscripts
spell the name in different ways.

26. It probably refers to a sacred plant identified by Yule with sweet
basil *(Ocymum sanctum),* an object of veneration in the region.

the fields, and cast them to the beasts and birds to be devoured. And they have here very fine oxen, which have horns a good half pace in length [girth?], and have a hump on the back like a camel. And from this city to Panche [Paroche?] is fourteen days' journey.]27 And it was in this place called Tana, as I have said before, that the four Minor Friars suffered a glorious martyrdom for the faith of Christ, and it took place after the manner following.

6. History of the martyrdom of the four friars in the city of Tana.28

When the friars aforesaid were at Ormes they made a bargain for a certain ship to take them to Polumbum,29 but

27. The parts relating to the customs of the Tana area do not appear in most of the manuscripts of the *Relatio*.

28. The martyrdom of the four Franciscan brothers — Thomas of Tolentino, James of Padua, Peter of Sienna, and Demetrius — is also recounted in some letters by Jordan of Sévérac and by Francis of Pisa, monks in Tabriz and Soltaniyeh. Their martyrdom would have occurred in April of 1321.

29. Modern Quilon, not far from the southern extremity of the Indian peninsula.

being once on board they were taken against their will to Tana. Here there be fifteen houses of Christians, that is to say of Nestorians, who are schismatics and heretics. And the friars having thus come hither, found harbor in the house of one of those Christians. And whilst they were staying there, one day there arose a quarrel between the good man of the house and his wife, and in the evening he gave her a sound beating. And in the morning the woman went and made a complaint of the beating to the *Cadi*, i.e., in their tongue the Bishop. And the Cadi having asked her if she had any proof of what she alleged, she answered that she could well prove it. "For," quoth she, "there were four Frank Rabbans"[30] (which is to say in our tongue four men of a religious order) "there in the house when he handled me thus. Question them and they will tell you the truth." And when the woman said this, there was a certain man of Alexandria there present who begged the Cadi to send for them, saying that they were men of great learning and knowledge in the Scriptures, and that it would be good to have a dispute with them concerning religion. The Cadi, hearing this, sent for them. And so when those

30. "Rabban," or "master," was the appellative used by the Syrian church to designate a monk.

brethren were brought before him, to wit, Friar Thomas of Tolentino in the March of Ancona, Friar James of Padua, and Friar Demetrius, a Georgian lay brother good at the tongues (Friar Peter of Sienna being left at home to take care of their things), the Cadi began at once to dispute with them about our Faith. And when the infidels disputed with them in this manner, alleging that Christ was mere man and not God, Friar Thomas took it in hand, and proved by arguments and instances that He was God and Man in one, and so confounded the Saracens that they were absolutely unable to maintain the contrary.

7. The same continued.

Then the Cadi, seeing himself thus put to confusion by them before the whole people, began to call out with a loud voice: "But what sayest thou of Machomet? What sayest thou of Machomet?" For such is the wont of the Saracens, that when they cannot maintain their cause with arguments, they take to maintaining it with swords and fists. And as the Cadi thus questioned Friar Thomas, the brethren answered saying: "We have proved to thee by arguments and instances that Christ who delivered a religion to the world was true God and Man, and since him Machomet hath come and hath delivered a religion which is contrary to the former. If thou be wise then well mayst thou know what to think of him." Then the Cadi and the other Saracens only shouted the louder: "But again what sayest thou of Machomet?" Then Friar Thomas replied: "Since ye can only repeat *What do I say of him,* I should blush to refuse the reply ye seek. I reply then, and tell you that Machomet is the son of perdition, and hath his place in hell with the devil his father, and not he only but all such as follow and keep his law, false as it is, and pestilent and accursed, hostile to God and the salvation of souls." And when the Saracens heard this they all began to shout with a loud voice together: "Let him die; let him die, for he hath blasphemed the Prophet!" And then they took the friars and bound them there in the sun, that they might die a dreadful death by the intense heat. For there the heat is so great that if one shall stand [bareheaded] in the sun for the space of a single mass he will die outright. Yet there they abode in the sun praising and glorifying God from the third until the ninth hour, cheerful and unscathed. And when the Saracens saw this they took counsel together, and came to the brethren, saying: "We mean to kindle a great blazing fire, and to cast you into it. And if the doctrine ye hold be true the fire will not burn you, but if it be false and evil ye shall be utterly consumed."

Then the brethren answered, saying: "We are ready, O Cadi, to go into the fire and into prison, or to endure whatever thou canst inflict on us for our religion; and ready thou shalt ever find us. But this one thing thou oughtest to know, that if the fire consume us, think not this cometh from (the fault of) our religion, but only from our sins, seeing that on account of our sins God may well let us burn. And for all that, our religion is not the less good and perfect as anything in the world ever can be; nor is there in the world any other faith whereby men may be saved but this."

8. The same history continued.

And as order was thus being taken for the burning of the friars, the report thereof spread like lightning throughout the whole city; and from the said city great and small, men and women, flocked together to see what should come of it. But the brethren were meanwhile brought out to the *Medan* i.e., the piazza of the city, where an exceeding great fire had been kindled. And Friar Thomas went forward to cast himself into the fire, but as he did so a certain Saracen caught him by the hood, saying: "Nay, thou shalt not go, for thou art old, and mayest have upon thee some crafty device whereby the fire could not burn thee; so let another than thou go in!" Then incontinently four Saracens laid violent hands on Friar James of Padua in order to cast him into the fire; but he said to them, "Suffer me and I will of my own free will cast myself in." But they, heeding not what he said, straightway threw him into it. And when they had done so, and he was there abiding in the fire, it blazed so high and far abroad that no one was able to see him, but they heard his voice continually invoking the name of the Blessed Virgin. And when the fire was quite spent, there was Friar James standing on the embers, joyous and exultant, with his hands raised to heaven making the sign of the cross, and with sound mind and pure heart praising the Lord without ceasing. And though the fire had been so great the slightest hurt or burn could not be found upon him. And when the people saw this they began to call out with one consent, "They are saints! They are saints! 'Tis sin to do them hurt. And we see that in truth their religion is good and holy." And when they had said thus, Friar James was called forth from the fire, and came out sound and unhurt. And when the Cadi saw this, he too began to cry out, saying: "He is no saint! He is no saint! But the reason why he is not burnt is that he hath on his back a garment from the land of Abraham. Wherefore let him be stript naked and so cast into the fire!"

And that this might be done effectually then came some villains of Saracens, and kindled a fire twice as great as before. And then they stript Friar James, and washed him, and anointed him copiously with oil, and that the fire might blaze more fiercely and burn up the friar the faster, they poured great quantities of oil upon the pile of wood, and then flung Friar James with a forcible fling into the middle of it. And the Friars Thomas and Demetrius abode without upon their knees, engaged fervently and instantly in prayer. And thus also Friar James came forth a second time without hurt as he had done before.

9. The same history continued.

And when the people saw this they shouted again with one consent: "'Tis a sin! 'Tis a sin to hurt them, for saints they be!" And so there was a very great noise among the people. And on seeing this second miracle the *Melic,* i.e., the podesta of the city, called to him Friar James, and made him put on his clothes, and said: "Go, brethren, with the grace of God, for ye shall suffer no harm at our hands. For we see well that ye are good and holy men; and that your religion is good and holy and true, we see past question. But to provide the better for your safety we counsel you to quit this place as speedily as ye may; for the Cadi will do his uttermost and spare no pains to take your lives."

While he was thus speaking it was about the hour of complines, and the whole people, idolaters and others, were standing about in a state of awe and astonishment, saying: "We have seen, from these men things so great and marvellous, that we know not what law we ought to follow and keep." And as they thus spake, the Melic caused those three friars to be taken and conveyed away across a certain arm of the sea that was at a little distance from the city, and where there was a certain suburb, whither the man in whose house they had been lodged accompanied them, and so they found harbor in the house of a certain idolater. And whilst they abode there the Cadi went to the Melic and said: "What are we about? For the law of Machomet is going to destruction unless something else be done. For these Frank Rabbans will now go preaching through the whole country, and as they have done such great marvels here which the whole of the people have seen, all will be converted to them, and so the law of Machomet will lose all power. And that this be not so there is a thing you ought to consider, and that is that Machomet hath ordered in the Alchoran (i.e., in his law) that if any one shall slay a Christian he shall have as much merit as if he had gone to Mecha." (Now ye must know, that Alchoran is the law of the Saracens as the Gospel is the law of the Christians; and Mecha is the place where Machomet is buried, and the Saracens go there on pilgrimage just as Christians go to the Sepulcher.)

Then the Melic answered the Cadi: "Go then and do as thou wilt."

10. The same history continued.

And when he had thus spoken the Cadi immediately took four armed men and sent them to slay the friars. But by the time these men had crossed the water it was night, and so at that late hour they could not find them. And now the Melic caused all the Christians who were in the city to be seized and put in prison. But when midnight was come the friars got up to say matins, and so the men who had been sent to slay them discovered where they were, and took them away outside the town beneath a certain tree, and said to them: "Ye must know that we have orders from the Cadi and the Melic to slay you; and we are reluctant to do it, for ye are good and holy men. But we cannot do otherwise. For if we do not their behests we and all our children and our wives shall die!" And the friars answered them, saying: "Since ye come hither that we through death temporal may attain to life eternal, do that which ye are bidden. For we are ready to bear manfully whatever tortures ye may inflict on us for our religion and for the love of Jesus Christ our Lord." And when they answered with this boldness and constancy, that Christian who had joined their company got into deep altercation with those four evil men. For he spake to them in this wise, saying: "Had I but a sword I would hinder your doing this, or ye should slay me along with them." Then they caused the friars to strip. And straightway Friar Thomas, joining his hands in the sign of the cross, suffered first, his head being cut off. And one of them then smote Friar James on the head and clove him to the eyes, and then immediately cut his head off. Friar Demetrius also first received a desperate stab in the breast and then his head was cut off. And as they thus rendered their souls to God in martyrdom, straightway the air was illuminated, and it became so bright that all were stricken with amazement, and at the same time the moon waxed wonderfully light and lustrous. And after this there were so great thunderings, lightnings, and flashings of fire, that almost all thought their end was come. And that ship which ought to have taken them to Polumbum, but carried them to Tana against their will, went to the bottom, so that nothing ever was known of her or her crew.

11. The same continued.

And in the morning the Cadi sent to the house to take possession of the friars' gear; they found there Peter of Sienna, the comrade of the other three friars, and took him to the Cadi. So the Cadi and other Saracens addressed him, and made him promises of great things if he would deny the faith, and confess that of Machomet. But he only ridiculed them and scorned their proposals in a way that made them marvel. So they began torturing him, and did so from morning until noon with sundry kinds of tortures. But he remained ever unshaken and firm in the faith, and manfully demolishing their doctrine, and showing it to be false. And when the Saracens saw that he was not to be turned from his purpose, they hung him up to a certain tree, and there he remained from the ninth hour until night. But when night fell they took him down from the tree quite unhurt, and when they saw it was so, they clove him asunder, and in the morning no trace of him was to be found. But it was revealed to a person worthy of belief that God had concealed his body till in due season He should be pleased to disclose it.

And that God might make manifest that their souls had inherited the kingdom of heaven, on that very day when these blessed friars became glorious martyrs, that Melic had fallen asleep, and as he thus lay asleep, lo! there appeared to him those glorious martyrs bright and shining like the sun, and holding swords in their hands, which they brandished over the Melic in such a way as if they would have cloven him asunder. And at this sight the Melic began to roar out, and with his noise brought his whole family running to see what ailed him, and what he would have. And he told them in reply: "Those Frank Rabbans whom I have caused to be slain have come hither with swords to slay me!" And so he sent for the Cadi, to whom he told what had befallen him, and asked his counsel as to what should be done in the matter, for he was convinced that he should perish utterly at their hands. Then the Cadi advised him that he should do some great work of charity on their account, if he would escape from the hands of those murdered men. So he sent straightway for the Christians whom he held in durance, and humbly asked their pardon for what he had caused to be done to them, behaving to them like a fellow and a brother. And besides he ordered that any one who should hurt any of the Christians in future should suffer death. Afterwards also the Melic caused four mosques, i.e., churches, to be built in honor of the friars, and put Saracen priests in each of them to abide continually.

12. The same history continued.

And when the emperor of Dili heard that those friars had undergone such a sentence, he sent and ordered the Melic to be seized and despatched to his presence with his hands bound. Being thus brought before the emperor, and questioned why he had so cruelly put those friars to death, he replied: "I suffered them to die because they sought to overthrow our law, and blasphemed the Prophet." Then the emperor said to him: "Most cruel hound, when thou sawest that God had twice delivered them from the fire,

how couldst thou dare thus to inflict death upon them?"
And having spoken thus, he ordered him with his whole
family to be cut in pieces. Such a death therefore as he
caused those brethren to undergo to their glory, he himself had now to undergo to his own damnation. And the
Cadi hearing of this fled from the city, and from the emperor's dominions.

Now in that country it is the custom never to bury the
dead, but bodies are only cast out in the fields, and thus
are speedily destroyed and consumed by the excessive heat.
So the bodies of these friars lay for fourteen days in the
sun, and yet were found quite fresh and undecayed as if on
the very day of their glorious martyrdom. And the Christians who were in that place seeing this took the bodies,
and caused them to be committed to the tomb.

13. How Fr. Odoric took up the bones of the four friars; and the wonders wrought thereby.

Then I, Friar Odoric, came into those regions, having
heard of their glorious martyrdom, and opening their
tombs I humbly and devoutly took up their bones. And as
God ofttimes worketh great marvels by means of his

saints, through these also it pleased him to work power-
fully. Thus when I had taken their bones, and wrapped
them in fair napkins, and accompanied by one brother of
the order and a servant, I was taking them to the house of
our friars at a certain place in Upper India,[31] I chanced to
lodge in the house of a certain man, and when I went to
sleep I placed those bones, or sacred relics rather as I
would call them, under my head. And as I thus slept the
house was suddenly set fire to by the Saracens, that they
might bring about my death by acclamation of the people.
For this is the emperor's command, that any whose house
is burnt shall suffer death. The house then being on fire
my comrade and the servant made their escape from it,
leaving me in it with those bones. And I took the bones of
the brethren, and seeking help from God I crouched into a
corner of the burning house. And three corners thereof
were consumed, and that one only was left in which I was
abiding. And as I sat there the fire was over my head, doing
me no harm and not burning the corner of the house.
And as long as I continued there with the bones, the fire
never came lower but hung over me like an atmosphere.

31. Odoric designated southern China with the name "Upper India."

But as soon as I quitted the house it was entirely destroyed and many others adjoining besides. And so I escaped unscathed.

14. The same continued.

Another such thing happened to me also on that journey. For as I went by sea with those bones, towards a certain city called Polumbum (where groweth the pepper in great store), the wind failed us utterly. Then the idolaters came beseeching their gods to give them a fair wind; which, however, was all to no purpose. Next came the Saracens, and wrought greatly to have a wind granted to them; but neither had they anything for all their prayers. Whereupon they enjoined on my comrade and me that we should pour forth our prayers to our God to bestow it upon us. And if this took effect the greatest honor would be shown us. And the skipper said to me, speaking in the Armenian tongue, that others might not understand: "If we cannot have a wind we shall cast those bones of yours into the sea." Then my comrade and I made prayers to God Himself, but seeing that still there was no wind to be had we began to promise ever so many masses in honor of the

Blessed Virgin if we could but have a wind; but even so we could not obtain any wind at all. So then I took one of those bones and gave it to our servant, and told him to go to the bow of the ship with haste and cast it into the sea; Then when the bone was so cast into the sea, straightway a most favorable wind arose which never failed until it brought us into harbor; and thus we got thither safely through the merits of those friars.

15. The same continued.

And when we were there in harbor at Polumbum we embarked on board another ship called a junk, and went as has already been said to Upper India, to a certain city called Zayton, in which our friars have two houses, in order there to deposit those sacred relics. Now on board that ship there were a good seven hundred souls, what with sailors and with merchants. And the idolaters have this custom, that before they enter port they make search throughout the whole vessel to ascertain what is on board; and if any dead men's bones should be found they would straightway cast them into the sea, for they say that to have such things on board involves great peril of death.

Though they did accordingly make this diligent search, and though the bones were there in a great quantity, yet they never did get any inkling of them. And so by God's permission we brought them safely to the house of our brethren, and there they were worthily deposited with honor and great worship. And by means of these sainted friars doth Almighty God still work many other wonders; and this is held true by both Pagans and Saracens. For when they are caught by any disease, they go and take of the earth of the place where the friars were slain, and wash it in water, and then drink the water, and so are immediately freed from all their ailments.

16. Fr. Odoric is done with the four friars; and now he telleth of the kingdom of Minibar and how pepper is got.

And now that ye may know how pepper is got, let me tell you that it groweth in a certain empire whereunto I came to land, the name whereof is Minibar,[32] and it groweth

32. A reference to the Malabar region, on the southwest coast of the Indian peninsula.

nowhere else in the world but there. And the forest in which the pepper groweth extendeth for a good eighteen days' journey, and in that forest there be two cities, the one whereof is called Flandrina and the other Cyngilin.[33] In the city of Flandrina some of the inhabitants are Jews and some are Christians; and between those two cities there is always internal war, but the result is always that the Christians beat and overcome the Jews.

Now, in this country they get the pepper in this manner. First, then, it groweth on plants which have leaves like ivy, and these are planted against tall trees, as our vines are here, and bear fruit just like bunches of grapes; and this fruit is borne in such quantities that they seem like to break under it. And when the fruit is ripe it is of a green color, and 'tis gathered just as grapes are gathered at the vintage, and then put in the sun to dry. And when it is dried it is stored in jars [and of the fresh pepper also they make a confection, of which I had to eat, and plenty of it]. And in this forest also there be rivers in which be many evil croco-

33. The city of Flandrina, which has now disappeared, was also noted by other travellers and geographers and must have been located on the coast, north of Calicut. As to Cyngliln, it has not been identified with certainty; according to Yule, it would be placed at Cranganur, about a hundred kilometers south of Calicut.

diles, i.e. serpents. [And there be many other kinds of serpents in the forest, which the men burn by kindling tow and straw, and so they are enabled to go safely to gather pepper.] [And here there be lions in great numbers, and a variety of beasts which are not found in our Frank countries. And here they burn the brazil-wood for fuel, and in the woods are numbers of wild peacocks.][34]

At the extremity of that forest, towards the south, there is a certain city which is called Polumbum, in which is grown better ginger than anywhere else in the world. And the variety and abundance of wares for sale in that city is so great that it would seem past belief to many folk.

17. Fr. Odoric discourseth of the manners of the idolaters of Polumbum.

[Here all the people go naked, only they wear a cloth just enough to cover their nakedness, which they tie behind.] All the people of this country worship the ox for their god [and they eat not his flesh]; for they say that he is, as

34. Some of the information about the fruits and animals of the Indian forest is found only in certain manuscripts of the *Relatio*.

it were, a sacred creature. Six years they make him to work for them, and the seventh year they give him rest from all labor, and turn him out in some appointed public place, declaring him thenceforward to be a consecrated animal. And they observe the following abominable superstition. Every morning they take two basins of gold or silver, and when the ox is brought from the stall they put these under him and catch his urine in one and his dung in the other. With the former they wash their faces, and with the latter they daub themselves, first on the middle of the forehead; secondly, on the balls of both cheeks; and, lastly, in the middle of the chest. And when they have thus anointed themselves in four places they consider themselves to be sanctified (for the day). Thus do the common people; and thus do the king and queen likewise.

They worship also another idol, which is half man and half ox. And this idol giveth responses out of its mouth, and ofttimes demandeth the blood of forty virgins to be given to it. For men and women there vow their sons and their daughters to that idol, just as here they vow to place them in some religious order. And in this manner many perish.

And many other things are done by that people which it would be abomination even to write or to hear of, and many other things be there produced and grown, which it booteth little to relate. But the idolaters of this realm have one detestable custom (that I must mention). For when any man dies, they burn him, and if he leave a wife they burn her alive with him, saying that she ought to go and keep her husband company in the other world. But if the woman have sons by her husband she may abide with them, if she will. And, on the other hand, if the wife die there is no law to impose the like on him; but he, if he likes, can take another wife. It is also customary there for the women to drink wine and not the men. The women also have their foreheads shaven, whilst the men shave not the beard. And there be many other marvellous and beastly customs which 'tis just as well not to write.

18. Concerning the kingdom of Mobar, where lieth the body of St. Thomas.

From this realm 'tis a journey of ten days to another realm which is called Mobar,[35] and this is very great, and hath

35. Mobar or Maabar was probably located near the southern tip of the peninsula or along its southwest coast. The tomb of Saint Thomas,

under it many cities and towns. And in this realm is laid
the body of the Blessed Thomas the Apostle. His church
is filled with idols, and beside it are some fifteen houses
of the Nestorians, that is to say, Christians, but vile and
pestilent heretics. There is likewise in this kingdom a certain wonderful idol, which all the provinces of India
greatly revere. It is as big as St. Christopher is commonly
represented by the painters, and it is entirely of gold,
seated on a great throne, which is also of gold. And round
its neck it hath a collar of gems of immense value. And
the church of this idol is also of pure gold, roof (and
walls) and pavement. People come to say their prayers to
the idol from great distances, just as Christian folk go
from far on pilgrimage to St. Peter's. And the manner of
those who come is thus: Some travel with a halter round
their necks; and some with their hands upon a board,
which is tied to their necks; others with a knife stuck in
the arm, which they never remove until they arrive before
the idol, so that the arm is then all infected. And some
have quite a different way of going. For these as they start
from their houses take three steps, and at the fourth they

which Odoric made quick reference to, was located near Madras, according to tradition.

make a prostration at full length upon the ground. And then they take a thurible and incense the whole length of that prostration. And thus they do continually until they reach the idol, so that sometimes when they go through this operation it taketh a very great while before they do reach the idol. But when those who are going along in this way wish to turn aside to do anything, they make a mark there to show how far they have gone, and so they (come back upon this, and) continue until they reach the idol.

19. Concerning other customs of the idolaters.

And hard by the church of this idol there is a lake, made by hand, into which the pilgrims who come thither cast gold or silver or precious stones, in honor of the idol, and towards the maintenance of the church, so that much gold and silver and many precious stones have been accumulated therein. And thus when it is desired to do any work upon the church, they make search in the lake and find all that hath been cast into it.

But annually on the recurrence of the day when that idol was made, the folk of the country come and take it down, and put it on a fine chariot; and then the king and queen and all the pilgrims, and the whole body of the people, join together and draw it forth from the church with loud singing of songs and all kinds of music; and many maidens go before it by two and two chanting in a marvellous manner. And many pilgrims who have come to this feast cast themselves under the chariot, so that its wheels may go over them, saying that they desire to die for their god. And the car passes over them, and crushes and cuts them asunder, and so they perish on the spot. And after this fashion they drag the idol to a certain customary place, and then they drag him back to where he was formerly, with singing and playing as before. And thus not a year passes but there perish more than five hundred men in this manner; and their bodies they burn, declaring that they are holy, having thus devoted themselves to death for their god.

And another custom they have of this kind. One will come saying: "I desire to sacrifice myself for my god." And then his friends and kinsfolk, and all the players of the country, assemble together to make a feast for him who is determined to die for his god. And they hang round his neck five very sharp knives, and lead him thus to the presence of the idol with loud songs. Then he takes one of those sharp knives and calls out with a loud voice,

"Thus I cut my flesh for my god"; and cutting a piece of his flesh wherever he may choose, he casteth it in the face of the idol; and saying again, "I devote myself to die for my god," he endeth by slaying himself there. And straightway they take his body and burn it, for they look on him as a saint, having thus slain himself for his idol. And many other things greatly to be marvelled at are done by these people, which are by no means to be written.

But the king of this island or province is passing rich in gold and silver and precious stones. And in this island are found as great store of good pearls as in any part of the world. And so of many other things which are found in this island, which it would take too long to write.

20. Concerning the country called Lamori, where the pole star is hidden; and also of Sumoltra.[36]

Departing from this region towards the south across the Ocean Sea, I came in fifty days to a certain country called

36. The land of Lamori, according to the commentators, formed the northwestern part of the island of Sumatra; Odoric will speak of it (with the name Sumoltra) at the end of the chapter.

Lamori, in which I began to lose sight of the north star, as the earth intercepted it. And in that country the heat is so excessive that all folk there, both men and women, go naked, not clothing themselves in any wise. And they mocked much at me on this matter, saying that God made Adam naked, but I must needs go against His will and wear clothes. Now, in that country all the women be in common; and no one there can say, this is my wife, or this is my husband! But when a woman beareth a boy or a girl she giveth the child to whom she listeth of those with whom she hath consorted, and calleth him the father. The whole of the land likewise is in common; and no one can say with truth, this or that part of the land is mine. But they have houses of their own, and not in common.

It is an evil and a pestilent generation, and they eat man's flesh there just as we eat beef here. Yet the country in itself is excellent, and hath great store of flesh-meats, and of wheat and of rice; and they have much gold also, and lign-aloes, and camphor, and many other things which are produced there. And merchants come to this island from far, bringing children with them to sell like cattle to those infidels, who buy them and slaughter them in the shambles and eat them. And so with many other things both good and bad, which I have not written.

In this same island towards the south is another kingdom by name Sumoltra, in which is a singular generation of people; for they brand themselves on the face with a little hot iron in some twelve places; and this is done by men and women both. And these folk are always at war with the others who go naked. In this country there is great abundance of produce. [It is a great market for pigs and fowls and for butter and rice, and they have also the excellent fruit called *mussi.* And here also gold and tin are found in great abundance.]

And near this country is another realm called Resengo,[37] towards the south. Many things are there produced whereof I do not write.

21. The friar speaketh of the excellent island called Java.

In the neighborhood of that realm is a great island, Java by name, which hath a compass of a good three thousand

37. Yule identified this region with Rejang on the southern coast of the island of Sumatra. It is unlikely that Odoric reached this zone, but he was still able to talk about it through indirect knowledge.

miles. And the king of it hath subject to himself seven crowned kings. Now this island is populous exceedingly, and is the second best of all islands that exist. For in it grow camphor, cubebs, cardamoms, nutmegs, and many other precious spices. It hath also very great store of all victuals save wine.

The king of this island hath a palace which is truly marvellous. For it is very great, and hath very great stair-cases, broad and lofty, and the steps thereof are of gold and silver alternately. Likewise the pavement of the palace hath one tile of gold and the other of silver, and the wall of the same is on the inside plated all over with plates of gold, on which are sculptured knights all of gold, which have great golden circles round their heads, such as we give in these parts to the figures of saints. And these circles are all beset with precious stones. Moreover, the ceiling is all of pure gold, and to speak briefly, this palace is richer and finer than any existing at this day in the world.

Now the Great Khan of Cathay many a time engaged in war with this king; but this king always vanquished and got the better of him. And many other things there be which I write not.

22. Of the land called Thalamasim, and of the trees that give flour, and other marvels.

Near to this country is another which is called Panten, but others call it Thalamasyn,[38] the king whereof hath many islands under him. Here be found trees that produce flour, and some that produce honey, others that produce wine, and others a poison the most deadly that existeth in the world. For there is no antidote to it known except one; and that is that if any one hath imbibed that poison he shall take of *stercus humanum* and dilute it with water, and of this potion shall he drink, and so shall he be absolutely quit of the poison. [And the men of this country being nearly all rovers, when they go to battle they carry every man a cane in the hand about a fathom in length, and put into one end of it an iron bodkin poisoned with this poison, and when they blow into the cane, the bodkin flieth and striketh whom they list, and those who are thus stricken incontinently die.][39]

But, as for the trees that produce flour, 'tis after this

38. This region has not been placed with certainty, but it could have been intended as Borneo, or the peninsula of Malacca.

39. The description of the blowgun is not cited in the majority of the manuscripts of the *Relatio*.

fashion. These are thick, but not of any great height; they are cut into with an axe round about the foot of the stem, so that a certain liquor flows from them resembling size. Now this is put into bags made of leaves, and put for fifteen days in the sun; and after that space of time a flour is found to have formed from the liquor. This they steep for two days in sea-water, and then wash it with fresh water. And the result is the best paste in the world, from which they make whatever they choose, cates of sorts and excellent bread, of which I, Friar Odoric, have eaten: for all these things have I seen with mine own eyes. And this kind of bread is white outside, but inside it is somewhat blackish.

By the coast of this country towards the south is the sea called the Dead Sea, the water whereof runneth ever towards the south, and if any one falleth into that water he is never found more. [And if the shipmen go but a little way from the shore they are carried rapidly downwards and never return again, and no one knoweth whither they are carried, and many have thus passed away, and it hath never been known what became of them.]

In this country also there be canes or reeds like great trees, and full sixty paces in length.[40] There be also canes

40. Odoric is speaking of bamboo cane.

of another kind which are called *Cassan,* and these always grow along the ground like what we call dog's grass, and at each of their knots they send out roots, and in such wise extend themselves for a good mile in length. And in these canes are found certain stones which be such that if any man wear one of them upon his person he can never be hurt or wounded by iron in any shape, and so for the most part the men of that country do wear such stones upon them. And when their boys are still young they take them and make a little cut in the arm and insert one of these stones, to be a safeguard against any wound by steel. And the little wound thus made in the boy's arm is speedily healed by applying to it the powder of a certain fish.

And thus through the great virtue of those stones the men who wear them become potent in battle and great corsairs at sea. But those who from being shipmen on that sea have suffered at their hands, have found out a remedy for the mischief. For they carry as weapons of offense sharp stakes of very hard wood, and arrows likewise that have no iron on the points; and as those corsairs are but poorly armored the shipmen are able to wound and pierce them through with these wooden weapons, and by this device they succeed in defending themselves most manfully.

Of these canes called *Cassan* they make sails for their

ships, dishes, houses, and a vast number of other things of the greatest utility to them. And many other matters there be in that country which it would cause great astonishment to read or hear tell of; wherefore I care not to write them at present.

23. How the king of Zampa keepeth many elephants and many wives.

At a distance of many days from this kingdom is another which is called Zampa,[41] and 'tis a very fine country, having great store of victuals and of all good things. The king of the country, it was said when I was there, had, what with sons and with daughters, a good two hundred children; for he hath many wives and other women whom he keepeth. This king hath also fourteen thousand tame elephants, which he made to be kept and tended by his boors as here oxen and various other animals are kept in partnership. [And other folk keep elephants there just as commonly as we keep oxen here.]

41. The kingdom of Zampa or Champa was located on the coast of modern Vietnam.

And in that country there is one thing which is really wonderful. For every species of fish that is in the sea visits that country in such vast numbers that at the time of their coming the sea seems to consist of nothing else but fish. And when they get near the beach they leap ashore, and then the folk come and gather them as many as they list. And so these fish continue coming ashore for two or three days together. And then a second species of fishes comes and does the same as the first; and so with the other species each in turn and in order until the last; and this they do but once in the year. And when you ask the folk of that country how this comes about, they tell you in reply that the fish come and act in that fashion in order to pay homage to their emperor.

In that country also I saw a tortoise bigger in compass than the dome of St. Anthony's church in Padua. And many other like things be there, which unless they were seen would be past belief; wherefore I care not to write them.

When a married man dies in this country his body is burned, and his living wife along with it. For they say that she should go to keep company with her husband in the other world also.

24. Of the island of Nicoveran, where the men have dogs' faces.

Departing from that country and sailing towards the south over the Ocean Sea, I found many islands and countries, whereamong was one called Nicoveran.[42] And this is a great isle, having a compass of a good two thousand miles, and both the men and the women there have faces like dogs. And these people worship the ox as their god, wherefore they always wear upon the forehead an ox made of gold or silver, in token that he is their god. All the folk of that country, whether men or women, go naked, wearing nothing in the world but an handkerchief to cover their shame. They be stalwart men and stout in battle, going forth to war naked as they are with only a shield that covers them from head to foot. And if they hap to take any one in war who cannot produce money to ransom himself with, they do straightway eat him. But if they can get money from him, they let him go.

42. According to all the commentators, the islands of Nicobar are situated in the Indian Ocean, north of Sumatra. If this is correct, Odoric's account does not follow the chronological order of the journey here, because he should have first passed these islands before reaching Sumatra.

And the king of that country weareth round his neck a string of three hundred very big pearls, for that he maketh to his gods daily three hundred prayers. He carrieth also in his hand a certain precious stone called a ruby, a good span in length and breadth, so that when he hath this stone in his hand it shows like a flame of fire. And this, it is said, is the most noble and valuable gem that existeth at this day in the world, and the great emperor of the Tartars of Cathay hath never been able to get it into his possession either by force or by money, or by any device whatever. This king attends to justice and maintains it, and throughout his realm all men may fare safely. And there be many other things in this kingdom that I care not to write of.

25. Concerning the island of Silan, and the marvels thereof.

There is also another island called Silan,[43] which hath a compass of good two thousand miles. There be found

43. The island of Sri Lanka. The account continues on here in a non-chronological order, because an eventual stop on the island would come up only after passing southern India.

therein an infinite number of serpents, and many other wild animals in great numbers, especially elephants. In this country also there is an exceeding great mountain, of which the folk relate that it was upon it that Adam mourned for his son one hundred years. In the midst of this mountain is a certain beautiful level place, in which there is a lake of no great size, but having a great depth of water. This they say was derived from the tears shed by Adam and Eve; but I do not believe that to be the truth, seeing that the water naturally springs from the soil.

The bottom of this pool is full of precious stones, and the water greatly aboundeth in leeches. The king taketh not those gems for himself, but for the good of his soul once or twice a year he suffereth the poor to search the water, and take away whatever stones they can find. But that they may be able to enter the water in safety they take lemons and bruise them well, and then copiously anoint the whole body therewith, and after that when they dive into the water the leeches do not meddle with them. And so it is that the poor folk go down into the pool and carry off precious stones if they can find them.

The water which comes down from the mountain issues forth by this lake. And the finest rubies are dug there; good diamonds too are found and many other good stones. And where that water descends into the sea there be found fine pearls. Wherefore the saying goes that this king hath more precious stones than any other king in the world. In this island there be sundry kinds of animals, both of birds and other creatures; and the country folk say that the wild beasts never hurt a foreigner, but only those who are natives of the island. There be also certain birds as big as geese, which have two heads. And this island hath also great store of victuals, and of many other good things whereof I do not write.

26. Of the island called Dondin and the evil manners there.

Departing from that island and going towards the south, I landed at a certain great island which is called Dondin,[44]

44. The island of Dondin has not been identified. Yule proposed an identification with the Andaman Islands, north of the Nicobar Islands. There is, however, little to support such a hypothesis. This chapter, which is one of the most unusual in the *Relatio,* has been considered by some to be a figment of the imagination. Still others have assigned to it symbolic value, like a summa of the moral monstrosities practiced by the pagans in the regions of India.

and this signifieth the same as "Unclean." They who dwell in that island are an evil generation, who devour raw flesh and every other kind of filth. They have also among them an abominable custom; for the father will eat the son, the son the father, the wife will eat the husband, or the husband the wife. And 'tis in this way: Suppose that the father of some one is ill. The son goeth then to the astrologer or priest (for 'tis the same), and sayeth thus: "Sir, go, I pray, and inquire of our god whether my father shall be healed of this infirmity or shall die of it." Then the priest and he whose father is ill go both unto the idol, which is made of gold or silver, and make a prayer to it, and say: "Lord, thou art our god! and as our god we adore thee! Answer to that we ask of thee! Such an one is ailing grievously; must he die, or shall he be delivered from his ailment? We ask thee!" Then the demon replies by the mouth of the idol, and says: "Thy father shall not die, but shall be freed from that ailment. And thou must do such and such things and so he shall recover." And so the demon shows the man all that he is to do for his father's recovery; and he returneth to his father accordingly, and tendeth him diligently until he be entirely recovered. But if the demon reply that the father will die, then the priest goeth to him and putteth a linen cloth over his mouth, and so suffocateth him and he dieth. And when they have thus slain him, they cut him in pieces, and invite all their friends and relations and all the players of the country round about to come to the eating of him, and eat him they do, with singing of songs and great merry-making. But they save his bones and bury them underground with great solemnity. And any of the relatives who have not been invited to this wedding feast (as it were) deem themselves to have been grievously slighted.

I rebuked these people sharply for so acting, saying to them: "Why do ye act thus against all reason? Why, were a dog slain and put before another dog he would by no means eat thereof; and why should you do thus, who seem to be men endowed with reason?" And their answer was: "We do this lest the flesh of the dead should be eaten of worms; for if the worms should eat his flesh his soul would suffer grievous pains; we eat his flesh therefore that his soul suffer not." And so, let me say what I would, they would not believe otherwise nor quit that custom of theirs.

27. A word in brief of India and the isles thereof.

And there be many other strange things in those parts which I write not, for unless a man should see them he never could believe them. For in the whole world there be no such marvels as in that realm (of India). What things I have written are only such as I was certain of, and such as I cannot doubt but they are as I have related them.

And as regards this India I have inquired from many who have knowledge of the matter, and they all assured me as with one voice that it includeth in its limits a good twenty-four thousand islands, in which there are sixty-four crowned kings. And the greater part of these islands is well peopled. So here I have done with this India, and will say no more thereof; but I will now tell you somewhat of Upper India.

28. Friar Odoric cometh to Upper India and the province of Manzi, and discourseth of them.

Ye shall know then that after I had sailed eastward over the Ocean Sea for many days I came to that noble province Manzi, which we call Upper India.[45] And as to that India

45. Odoric divided China into two very distinct districts: a southern district, Manzi (Man-tsu), also called "Upper India," and a northern one, Cathay.

I made diligent inquiry from Christians, Saracens, and idolaters, and from all the Great Khan's officers, and they all told me, with one consent as it were, that the province of Manzi hath two thousand great cities; cities I mean of such magnitude that neither Treviso nor Vicenza[46] would be entitled to be numbered among them. Indeed in that country the number of the people is so great that among us here it would be deemed incredible; [and in many parts I have seen the population more dense than the crowds you see at Venice on the Ascension Day]. And the land hath great store of bread, of wine, of rice, of flesh, and of fish of sorts, and of all manner of victuals whatever that are used by mankind. And all the people of this country are traders and artificers, and no man ever seeketh alms, however poor he be, as long as he can do anything with his own hands to help himself. [But those who are fallen into indigence and infirmity are well looked after and provided with necessaries.]

The men, as to their bodily aspect, are comely enough,

46. Treviso and Vicenza, like Padua, Bologna, and Ferrara (all of which are referred to elsewhere), are cities in northeastern Italy, Odoric's home region, where the first recipients of his travel account also lived.

but colorless, having beards of long straggling hairs like mousers — cats I mean. And as for the women, they are the most beautiful in the world!

29. Of the great city Censcalan.

The first city to which I came in this country was called Censcalan,[47] and 'tis a city as big as three Venices. It is one day's voyage from the sea, standing upon a certain river, the water whereof is derived from the sea, and extendeth twelve days' journey into the land. The whole population of this city, as well as of all Manzi and Upper India, worship idols. And this city hath shipping so great and vast in amount that to some it would seem well nigh incredible. Indeed all Italy hath not the amount of craft that this one city hath. And here you can buy three hundred pounds of fresh ginger for less than a groat! The geese too are bigger and finer and cheaper than anywhere in the world. For one of them is as big as two of ours, and 'tis all white as milk, but has a bone on the top of its head about the size of an egg, which is of a blood color;

47. Today's Guangzhou (Canton).

whilst under its throat it has a skin hanging down for half a span. And these geese are as fat as fat can be, yet one of them well dressed and seasoned you shall have there for less than a groat. And as it is with the geese, so also with the ducks and fowls; they are so big that you would think them perfectly marvellous.

Here too there be serpents bigger than anywhere else in the world, many of which are taken and eaten with great relish. These serpents [have quite a fragrant odor and] form a dish so fashionable that if a man were to give a dinner and not have one of these serpents on his table, he would be thought to have done nothing. In short this city hath a great abundance of all possible kinds of victual.

30. Concerning the noble city called Zayton; and how the folk thereof regale their gods.

Departing from that district, and passing through many cities and towns, I came to a certain noble city which is called Zayton,[48] where we Friars Minor have two houses;

48. The city of Zayton, a noteworthy port; in the fourteenth century it was also the see of a Catholic bishopric. It has not been posi-

and there I deposited the bones of our friars who suffered martyrdom for the faith of Jesus Christ.

In this city is great plenty of all things that are needful for human subsistence. For example, you can get three pounds and eight ounces of sugar for less than half a groat. The city is twice as great as Bologna, and in it are many monasteries of devotees, idol worshippers every man of them. In one of those monasteries which I visited there were three thousand monks and eleven thousand idols. And one of those idols, which seemed to be smaller than the rest, was as big as St. Christopher might be. I went thither at the hour fixed for feeding their idols, that I might witness it; and the fashion thereof is this: All the dishes which they offer to be eaten are piping hot so that the smoke riseth up in the face of the idols, and this they consider to be the idols' refection. But all else they keep for themselves and gobble up. And after such fashion as this they reckon that they feed their gods well.

The place is one of the best in the world, and that as regards its provision for the body of man. Many other

---

tively located but must have been somewhere near modern Zhangzhou (Amoy).

things indeed might be related of this place, but I will not write more about them at present.

31. The friar telleth of the city Fuzo and its marvels; also of rare fashions of fishing.

Thence I passed eastward to a certain city called Fuzo,[49] which hath a compass of a good thirty miles. And here be seen the biggest cocks in the world. And there be hens also that are white as snow, and have no feathers, but have wool only upon them, like sheep. The city is a mighty fine one, and standeth upon the sea.

Departing thence and travelling for eighteen days, I passed through many cities and towns, and witnessed a great variety of things. And as I travelled thus I came to a certain great mountain. And on the one side all the animals that dwell there are black, and the men and women have a very strange way of living. But on the other side all the animals are white and the men and women have a quite different way of living from the others. All the married women there wear on their heads a great barrel of horn, that they may be known to be married.

49. Today's Fuzhou, on the southeast coast of China.

Passing hence, and travelling for eighteen days more, through many cities and towns, I came to a certain great river,[50] and I tarried at a certain city [called Belsa] which hath a bridge across that river. And at the head of the bridge was a hostel in which I was entertained. And mine host, wishing to gratify me, said: "If thou wouldst like to see good fishing, come with me." And so he led me upon the bridge, and I looked and saw in some boats of his that were there certain waterfowl tied upon perches. And these he now tied with a cord round the throat that they might not be able to swallow the fish which they caught. Next he proceeded to put three great baskets into a boat, one at each end and the third in the middle, and then he let the waterfowl loose. Straightway they began to dive into the water, catching great numbers of fish, and ever as they caught them putting them of their own accord into the baskets, so that before long all the three baskets were full. And mine host then took the cord off their necks and let them dive again to catch fish for their own food. And when they had thus fed they returned to their perches and were tied up as before. And some of those fish I had for my dinner.

50. This could be the Fuchun Jiang River, at whose estuary the city of Hangzhou is situated.

After departing thence and travelling for many days, I witnessed another fashion of fishing. The men this time were in a boat, wherein they had a tub full of hot water; and they were naked, and had each of them a bag slung over his shoulder. Now they dived under water [for half a quarter of an hour or so], and caught the fish with their hands, stowing them in those bags that they had. And when they came up again they emptied the bags into the boat, whilst they, themselves got into the tub of hot water, and others went in their turn and did as the first; and so great numbers of fish were taken.

32. Concerning the city of Cansay, which is the greatest city on earth.

Departing thence, I came unto the city of Cansay,[51] a name which signifieth "the City of Heaven." And 'tis the greatest city in the whole world, [so great indeed that I should scarcely venture to tell of it, but that I have met at Venice people in plenty who have been there]. It is a good

51. Modern Hangzhou, which for a long time was the capital of China.

hundred miles in compass, and there is not in it a span of ground which is not well peopled. And many a tenement is there which shall have ten or twelve households comprised in it. And there be also great suburbs which contain a greater population than even the city itself. For the city hath twelve chief gates, and from each of them cities extend to a distance of some eight miles, each one greater than Venice is or Padua. So that you may for six or seven days travel continually about one of these suburbs, and yet shall you seem to have gone but a very little way.

This city is situated upon lagoons of standing water [with canals] like the city of Venice. And it hath more than twelve thousand bridges, on each of which are stationed guards guarding the city on behalf of the Great Khan. And at the side of this city there flows a river near which it is built like Ferrara by the Po, for it is longer than it is broad.

I made diligent inquiry regarding the city, and asked questions of Christians, Saracens, idolaters, and everybody else, and they all agreed as with one voice that it had a circuit of one hundred miles. And they have an edict from their Lord that every fire shall pay to the Great Khan annually a tax of one *balis*, i.e., of five pieces of paper like silk, a sum equal to one florin and a half. And their way of managing is this, that ten or twelve households will unite to have one fire, and so pay for one fire only. Now of these fires there are reckoned eighty-five *tumans,* and with four more of Saracens, making eighty-nine *tumans.* Now one tuman is equal to ten thousand fires. And besides these there are the Christians and the merchants and others only passing through the country.

This being so, I greatly marvelled how such numbers of human bodies could manage to dwell in one place, and yet there is always there great plenty of bread and pork, and rice and wine, which wine is otherwise called *Bigni,* and is reputed a noble drink; and indeed great abundance of all other victuals is found there.

33. Of the marvellous sight that Friar Odoric beheld in a certain monastery of the idolaters.

This is the royal city in which the king of Manzi formerly dwelt. And four of our friars that were in that city had converted a man that was in authority there, in whose house I was entertained. And he said to me one day: "*Atha* (which is to say *Father*), wilt thou come and see the place?" And when I said that I would willingly go, we got into a boat, and went to a certain great monastery of the people of the country [which was called Thebe]. And he called to him one of their monks, saying: "Seest here this *Franki Rabban?* (which meaneth this Frank monk). He cometh from where the sun sets; and goeth now to Cambalech to pray for the life of the Great Khan. Show him therefore, prithee, something worth seeing, so that if he get back to his own country he may be able to say, I have seen such and such strange things in Cansay!" And the monk replied that he would do so with pleasure.

So he took two great buckets full of scraps from the table, and opening the door of a certain shrubbery which was there we went therein. Now in this shrubbery there is a little hill covered with pleasant trees [and all full of grottoes]. And as we stood there he took a gong, and began to beat upon it, and at the sound a multitude of animals of divers kinds began to come down from the hill, such as apes, monkeys, and many other animals having faces like men, to the number of some three thousand, and took up their places round about him in regular ranks. And when they were thus ranged round about him, he put down the vessels before them and fed them as fast as he was able. And when they had been fed he began again to beat the gong, and all returned to their retreats. So I, laughing heartily, be-

129

gan to say: "Tell me, prithee, what this meaneth?" And he answered: "These animals be the souls of gentlemen, which we feed in this fashion for the love of God!" But quoth I: "No souls be these, but brute beasts of sundry kinds." And he said: "No, forsooth, they be nought else but the souls of gentlemen. For if a man be noble his soul entereth the form of some one of these noble animals; but the souls of boors enter the forms of baser animals and dwell therein!" And say what I list against it, nought else would he believe.

But if anyone should desire to tell all the vastness and great marvels of this city, a good quire of stationery would not hold the matter, I believe. For 'tis the greatest and noblest city, and the finest for merchandise, that the whole world containeth.

34. Of the city called Chilenfu, and of the great river Talay, and of certain Pygmies.

Departing from that city and travelling for six days, I arrived at another great city called Chilenfu,[52] the walls whereof have a circuit of forty miles. And in it there be

52. Today's Nanjing (Nanking).

some three hundred and sixty stone bridges, finer than the whole world can show. In this city was the first residence of the king of Manzi, where he used to dwell. It is very well peopled, and there is such an amount of craft thereat as is right marvellous to behold. The city is planted passing well, and hath great store of all good things.

And quitting this city, I came to a certain great river which is called Talay,[53] and this is the greatest river that exists in the world. For where it is narrowest it is some seven miles in width. And this river passeth through the land of the Pygmies, or Biduini, whose city is called Cathan,[54] and that is one of the best and finest cities in the world. These Pygmies are three spans in height, and they do greater work in cotton, as it is called, than any people in the world. And the full-sized men who dwell there beget sons who are more than half of them like those Pygmies who are so small. The women are wedded in their fifth year, and so there are born and begotten of these little people a countless number. These Pygmies,

53. Chang Liang River (Yang tze Kiang).

54. This city has not been positively identified, and it is not clear if Odoric truly visited here or simply described it from what he had heard.

both male and female, are famous for their small size. But they have rational souls like ourselves.

35. Concerning the cities of Iamzai and of Menzu.

And as I travelled upon this river Talay, I passed many cities and towns, and I came to a certain city called Iamzai,[55] at which our Minor Friars have a house. And here also be three churches of the Nestorians. This is a noble city, and hath a good forty-eight to fifty-eight tumans of fireplaces, every tuman being ten thousand. In this city are to be had in great abundance all kinds of things on which Christian people live. And the lord of this city hath from salt alone a revenue of five hundred tumans of balis; and a balis being worth a florin and a half, thus a tuman maketh fifteen thousand florins. But as a grace to this people the said lord made a remission to them of two hundred tumans, lest distress should be created.

There is a custom in this city that if any one desire to give a great dinner or entertainment to his friends he goes

55. Modern Yangzhou, where Marco Polo was governor for three years.

to one of the hostels which are established for this very purpose, and saith to the host thereof: "Make me a dinner for such a number of my friends, and I propose to expend such and such a sum upon it." Then the host does exactly as ordered, and the guests are better served than they would have been in the entertainer's own house.

This city hath also a vast amount of shipping. About ten miles from this city, towards the mouth of that great river Talay, there is a certain other city called Menzu.[56] This city hath shipping finer and more numerous peradventure than any other city in the world. And all the vessels are as white as snow, being coated with whitewash. And on board of them you find halls and taverns and many other conveniences, as handsome and well ordered as are anywhere to be found. Indeed it is something hard to believe when you hear of, or even when you see, the vast scale of the shipping in those parts.

56. This city, notwithstanding the precise geographic indication given ("towards the mouth of that great river Talay"), has not yet been accurately located. It could be Zhenjiang, situated at the point where the Chang Jiang intersects with the Great Imperial Canal. Yule, on the other hand, believed that Odoric had confused it with modern Ningbo, called in ancient times Mingchu, which is located much farther south. At the mouth of the river lies the city of Shanghai.

36. Of the river Caramoran; and of certain other cities visited by Friar Odoric.

Quitting that city and travelling by fresh water channels, I passed many cities and towns, and after eight days I came to a certain city named Lenzin, which standeth on a river called Caramoran.[57] This river passeth through the very midst of Cathay, and doth great damage to that country when it breaks its banks, just as the Po does by Ferrara. And as I travelled by that river towards the east, and passed many towns and cities, I came to a certain city which is called Sunzumayu,[58] which hath a greater plenty of silk than perhaps any other place an earth, for when silk there is at its dearest you can still have forty pounds for less than eight groats. There is in the place likewise great store of all kinds of merchandise, and likewise of bread and wine, and all other good things. [And seeing that there were in this place more people than I had seen

57. The city of Lenzin may be the modern city of Linqing, situated not far from the Huan River, here called by the Mongolian name Caramoran.

58. It has been proposed that today's Jining is the correct location for this city. Jining is halfway between Nanking and Peking. But, if so, this stop should have preceded that made in Lenzin.

in any other, when I asked how that came to pass, they told me that it was because the air of the place was so salubrious, insomuch that there were few that died of aught but old age.][59]

37. The friar reacheth Cambalech, and discourseth thereof, and of the Great Khan's palace there.

And departing thence, I passed on through many a city and many a town towards the east, until I came to that noble city Cambalech,[60] an old city of that famous province of Cathay. The Tartars took the city, and then built another at a distance of half-a-mile, which they called Taydo.

This latter city hath twelve gates, between every two of which there is a space of two long miles; and betwixt the two cities also there is a good amount of population, the compass of the two together being more than forty miles. Here the Great Khan hath his residence, and hath a great

59. The passage that speaks about the healthiness of the air and the longevity of the population is missing from the majority of the manuscripts of the *Relatio*.

60. Cambalech was modern Beijing (Peking), then the capital of China.

palace, the walls of which are some four miles in compass. And within this space be many other fine palaces. [For within the great palace wall is a second enclosure, with a distance between them of perhaps half a bowshot, and in the midst between those two walls are kept his stores and all his slaves; whilst within the inner enclosure dwells the Great Khan with all his family, who are most numerous, so many sons and daughters, sons-in-law, and grandchildren hath he; with such a multitude of wives and councillors and secretaries and servants, that the whole palace of four miles' circuit is inhabited.]

And within the enclosure of the great palace there hath been a hill thrown up on which another palace is built, the most beautiful in the whole world. And this whole hill is planted over with trees, wherefrom it hath the name of the *Green Mount.* And at the side of this hill hath been formed a lake [more than a mile round], and a most beautiful bridge built across it. And on this lake there be such multitudes of wild geese and ducks and swans, that it is something to wonder at; so that there is no need for that lord to go from home when he wisheth for sport. Also within the walls are thickets full of sundry sorts of wild animals; so that he can follow the chase when he chooses without ever quitting the domain.

But his own palace in which he dwells is of vast size and splendor. The basement thereof is raised about two paces from the ground, and within there be four-and-twenty columns of gold; and all the walls are hung with skins of red leather, said to be the finest in the world. In the midst of the palace is a certain great jar, more than two paces in height, entirely formed of a certain precious stone called *Merdacas,* [and so fine that I was told its price exceeded the value of four great towns]. It is all hooped round with gold, and in every corner thereof is a dragon represented as poised to strike most fiercely. And this jar hath also fringes of network of great pearls hanging therefrom, and these fringes are a span in breadth. Into this vessel drink is conveyed by certain conduits from the court of the palace; and beside it are many golden goblets from which those drink who list.

In the hall of the palace also are many peacocks of gold. And when any of the Tartars wish to amuse their lord, then they go one after the other and clap their hands; upon which the peacocks flap their wings, and make as if they would dance. Now this must be done either by diabolic art, or by some engine underground.

38. The friar setteth forth
the state of the Khan's court.

But when the Lord Khan is seated on his imperial throne, the queen is placed at his left hand; and a step lower are two others of his women; whilst at the bottom of the steps stand all the other ladies of his family. And all who are married wear upon their heads the foot of a man as it were, a cubit and a half in length, and at the top of that foot there are certain cranes' feathers, the whole foot being set with great pearls; so that if there be in the whole world any fine and large pearls they are to be found in the decorations of those ladies.

On the right hand of the king is placed his firstborn son that shall reign after him; and below stand all who are of the blood royal. And there be four scribes also, to take down all the words that the king may utter. And in front of the king stand his barons and others, an innumerable multitude, and nobody dares say a word unless the lord shall address him, except the jesters, who may say something to amuse their lord. But even they must not be bold enough to transgress the bounds which the king hath laid down for them.

And before the gates of the palace stand barons as

warders, to see that no one touch the threshold of the door; and if they catch anyone doing so they beat him soundly.

And when that great lord wishes to make an entertainment he shall have fourteen thousand barons with coronets on their heads waiting upon him at the banquet. And every one of them shall have a coat on his back such that the pearls on it alone are worth some fifteen thousand florins. And the court is ordered passing well, all being ranked by tens and hundreds and thousands, and all having their duties assigned, standing answerable one to another for any breach either to their own charges or in the charges of those subordinate to them.

I, Friar Odoric, was full three years in that city of his, and often present at those festivals of theirs; for we Minor Friars have a place assigned to us at the emperor's court, and we be always in duty bound to go and give him our benison. So I took the opportunity to make diligent inquiry from Christians, Saracens, and all kinds of idolaters, and likewise from our own converts to the faith, of whom there be some who are great barons at that court, and have to do with the king's person only. Now these all told me with one voice as follows: that the king's players alone amount to 13 tumans; that of those others who keep the dogs and wild beasts and fowls there be 15 tumans; of leeches to take charge of the royal person there be four hundred idolaters, eight Christians, and one Saracen. And all these have from the king's court whatever provision they require. [And there be never more nor fewer, but when one dies another is appointed in his place.] As for the rest of the establishment it is past counting. [In short, the court is truly magnificent, and the most perfectly ordered that there is in the world, with barons, gentlemen, servants, secretaries, Christians, Turks, and idolaters, all receiving from the court what they have need of.]

39. Of the order of the Great Khan when he journeyeth.

Now, this lord passeth the summer at a certain place which is called Sandu,[61] situated towards the north, and the coolest habitation in the world. But in the winter season he abideth in Cambalech. And when he will ride from the one place to the other this is the order thereof. He

61. Today, Shangdu in central Mongolia, approximately two hundred kilometers northwest of Peking.

hath four armies of horsemen, one of which goeth a day's march in front of him, one at each side, and one a day's march in rear, so that he goeth always, as it were, in the middle of a cross. And marching thus, each army hath its route laid down for it day by day, and findeth at its halts all necessary provender. But his own immediate company hath its order of march thus. The king travelleth in a two-wheeled carriage, in which is formed a very goodly chamber, all of lign-aloes and gold, and covered over with great and fine skins, and set with many precious stones. And the carriage is drawn by four elephants, well broken in and harnessed, and also by four splendid horses, richly caparisoned. And alongside go four barons, who are called *Cuthe*, keeping watch and ward over the chariot that no hurt come to the king. Moreover, he carrieth with him in his chariot twelve gerfalcons; so that even as he sits therein upon his chair of state or other seat, if he sees any birds pass he lets fly his hawks at them. And none may dare to approach within a stone's throw of the carriage, unless those whose duty brings them there. And thus it is that the king travelleth.

And so also his women travel, according to their degree; and his heir apparent travels in similar state.

As for the numbers which the lord hath with him on

his progress, 'tis difficult to believe or conceive of them. The number of the troops in those armies that attend the lord is fifty tumans, and these are entirely provided with everything by the lord. And if anyone happen to die of those who are enrolled among them, another instantly replaces him; so that the number is always complete.

40. The greatness of the Khan's dominion; and how hostels are provided therein; and how news are carried to the lord.

This empire hath been divided by the lord thereof into twelve parts; each one whereof is termed a *Singo.* And of those twelve parts that of Manzi forms one which hath under it two thousand great cities. And, indeed, so vast is that empire of his, that if one wished to visit each of these provinces he would have enough to do for six months; and that exclusive of the islands, five thousand in number, which are not comprehended in the number of the twelve provinces. [Moreover, there be four chief ministers to govern the empire of this great lord.]

And that travellers may have their needs provided for, throughout his whole empire he hath caused houses and courts to be established as hostelries, and these houses are called *yam.* In these houses is found everything necessary for subsistence, [and for every person who travels throughout those territories, whatever be his condition, it is ordained that he shall have two meals without payment]. And when any matter of news arises in the empire messengers start incontinently at a great pace on horseback for the court; but if the matter be very serious and urgent they set off upon dromedaries. And when they come near those yam, hostels or stations, they blow a horn, whereupon mine host of the hostel straightway maketh another messenger get ready; and to him the rider who hath come posting up delivereth the letter, whilst he himself tarrieth for refreshment. And the other taking the letter, maketh haste to the next yam, and there doth as did the first. And in this manner the emperor receiveth in the course of one natural day the news of matters from a distance of thirty days' journey.

But the despatch of foot runners is otherwise ordered. For certain appointed runners abide continually in certain station-houses called *chidebeo,* and these have a girdle with a number of bells attached to it. Now those stations are distant the one from the other perhaps three miles; and when a runner approaches one of those houses he causes those

bells of his to jingle very loudly; on which the other runner in waiting at the station getteth ready in haste, and
taking the letter hastens on to another station as fast as he
can. And so it goes from runner to runner until it reaches
the Great Khan himself. And so nothing can happen, in
short, throughout the whole empire, but he hath instantly,
or at least very speedily, full tidings thereof.

41. Concerning the Khan's great hunting matches.

When the Great Khan goes a hunting 'tis thus ordered. At
some twenty days' journey from Cambalech, there is a fine
forest of eight days' journey in compass; and in it are such
multitudes and varieties of animals as are truly wonderful.
All round this forest there be keepers posted on account of
the Khan, to take diligent charge thereof; and every third or
fourth year he goeth with his people to this forest. On such
occasions they first surround the whole forest with beaters,
and let slip the dogs and the hawks trained to this sport,
and then gradually closing in upon the game, they drive it
to a certain fine open spot that there is in the middle of the
wood. Here there becomes massed together an extraordinary multitude of wild beasts, such as lions, wild oxen,

bears, stags, and a great variety of others, and all in a state of the greatest alarm. For there is such a prodigious noise and uproar raised by the birds and the dogs that have been let slip into the wood, that a person cannot hear what his neighbor says; and all the [unfortunate] wild beasts quiver with terror at the disturbance. And when they have all been driven together into that open glade, the Great Khan comes up on three elephants and shoots five arrows at the game. As soon as he has shot, the whole of his retinue do likewise. And when all have shot their arrows (each man's arrows having a token by which they may be discerned), then the Great Emperor causeth to be called out "*Syo!*" which is to say as it were "Quarter!" to the beasts (to wit) that have been driven from the wood. Then [the huntsmen sound the recall, and call in the dogs and hawks from the prey, and] the animals which have escaped with life are allowed to go back into the forest, and all the barons come forward to view the game that has been killed and to recover the arrows that they had shot (which they can well do by the marks on them); and everyone has what his arrow has struck. And such is the order of the Khan's hunting.

42. Concerning the four great feasts
that the Khan keepeth.

Every year that emperor keepeth four great feasts, to wit, the day of his birth, that of his circumcision, and so forth. To these festivals he summons all his barons and all his players, and all his kinsfolk; and all these have their established places at the festival. But it is especially at the days of his birth and circumcision that he expects all to attend. And when summoned to such a festival all the barons come with their coronets on, whilst the emperor is seated on his throne as has been described above, and all the barons are ranged in order in their appointed places. Now these barons are arrayed in divers colors; for some, who are the first in order, wear green silk; the second are clothed in crimson; the third in yellow. And all these have coronets on their heads, and each holds in his hand a white ivory tablet and wears a golden girdle of half a span in breadth; and so they remain standing and silent. And round about them stand the players with their banners and ensigns. And in one corner of a certain great palace abide the philosophers, who keep watch for certain hours and conjunctions; and when the hour and conjunction waited for by the philosophers arrives, one of them calls out with a loud voice, saying, "Prostrate yourselves before the emperor our mighty lord!" And immediately all the barons touch the ground three times with their heads. Then he will call out again: "Rise, all of you!" and immediately they get up again. And then they wait for another auspicious moment, and when it comes he will shout out again, "Put your fingers in your ears!" and so they do. And then, "Take them out!" and they obey. And then they will abide awhile, and then he will say, "Bolt meal!" and so they go on with a number of other such words of command, which they allege to have a deep import. And there be also many officers to look diligently that none of the barons or of the players are absent. For any one of them who should absent himself would incur heavy penalties. And when the proper hour and moment for the players comes, then the philosophers say, "Make an entertainment for the lord!" and incontinently they all begin to play on their instruments of every kind, with such a clamor of music and song that 'tis enough to stun you. Then a voice is heard saying, "Silence all!" and they all cease. And after this all those of the famous princely families parade with white horses. And a voice is heard calling, "Such an one of such a family to present so many hundreds of white horses to the lord"; and then some of them come forward saying that they bring two hundred horses (say) to offer to the lord, which are ready before the palace. And 'tis something incredible the number of white horses which are presented to the lord on such an occasion. And then come barons to offer presents of different kinds on behalf of the other barons of the empire; and all the superiors of the monasteries likewise come with presents to the Khan, and are in duty bound to give him their benison. And this also do we Minor Friars. And when all this ceremony has been gone through, then come certain singing men before him, and also certain singing women who sing so sweetly that it is quite delightful to listen to them [and this pleased me most of all]. Then come mummers leading lions whom they pause to salute the lord with a reverence. And jugglers cause cups of gold full of good wine to fly through the air and offer themselves to the lips of all who list to drink of it. Such things and many more are done in that lord's presence. And any account that one can give of the magnificence of that lord, and of the things that are done in his court, must seem incredible to those who have not witnessed it.

But no one need wonder at his being able to maintain such an expenditure; for there is nothing spent as money in his whole kingdom but certain pieces of paper which are there current as money, whilst an infinite amount of treasure comes into his hands.

43. Concerning a certain melon that produceth a beast like a lamb.

Another passing marvellous thing may be related, which, however, I saw not myself, but heard from trustworthy persons. For 'tis said that in a certain great kingdom called Cadeli there be mountains called the Caspean Mountains, on which are said to grow certain very large melons. And when these be ripe, they burst, and a little beast is found inside like a small lamb, so that they have both melons and meat! And though some, peradventure, may find that hard to believe, yet it may be quite true; just as it is true that there be in Ireland trees which produce birds. [And here I would make an end of speaking of the Great Khan, for I am certainly unable to tell the thousandth part of what I have seen. In any case I think it best to pass to other matters.]⁶²

62. The final part of Odoric's account consists of different types of information, none of which is organized in any strict geographic or-

44. The friar, passing from Cathay, describeth sundry lands as of Prester John and others.

Departing from that land of Cathay and travelling westward for fifty days through many cities and towns, I arrived at the country of Prester John;[63] but as regards him not one hundredth part is true of what is told of him as if it were undeniable. His principal city is called Tozan, and chief city though it is, Vicenza would be reckoned its superior. He has, however, many other cities under him, and by a standing compact always receives to wife the Great Khan's daughter.

Travelling thence for many days, I came unto a certain province which is called Kansan,[64] and that is the second

der. The kingdom of Cadeli, which is spoken of at this point, would most likely have been located in the Caspian Mountains, namely, in the Caucasus region. The legend of the vegetable lamb would have fit into a popular Russian belief.

63. The kingdom of Prester John, the mysterious figure who, according to western tradition, was the leader of a powerful Christian state located east of the Muslim dominions. The commentators place it in central Mongolia. The city of Tozan, which would have been the capital of this kingdom, has never been positively identified.

64. In all probability, this is Shaanxi, which Odoric could have

best province in the world, and the best populated. For where it is most narrow it hath a width of fifty days' journey, and its length is more than sixty. And everywhere it has such a population that when you go forth from the gate of one city you already see the gate of another. And it hath also great store of victuals, but above all of chestnuts. Rhubarb likewise grows in this province, and that in such abundance that you may load an ass with it for less than six groats. And this province is one of the twelve divisions of the empire of the Great Khan.

45. Concerning the realm of Tibet, where dwelleth the Pope of the idolaters.

Quitting this province, I came to a certain great kingdom called Tibet,[65] which is on the confines of India Proper, and is subject to the Great Khan. They have in it great plenty of bread and wine as anywhere in the world. The

crossed in returning to Europe if he had followed the land route that went through the central Asian steppes and along the Black Sea.

65. Even allowing for a return journey by land for Odoric, it is not easy to believe that he went through Tibet, which lay much further south.

folk of that country dwell in tents made of black felt. But the chief and royal city is all built with walls of black and white, and all its streets are very well paved. In this city no one shall dare to shed the blood of any, whether man or beast, for the reverence they bear a certain idol which is there worshipped. In that city dwelleth the *Abassi*, i.e., in their tongue the Pope, who is the head of all the idolaters, and who has the disposal of all their benefices such as they are after their manner.

And the fashions of this kingdom are thus. The women have their hair plaited in more than one hundred tresses, and they have a couple of tusks as long as those of wild boars. And another fashion they have in this country is this. Suppose such an one's father to die, then the son will say, "I desire to pay respect to my father's memory"; and so he calls together all the priests and monks and players in the country round, and likewise all the neighbors and kinsfolk. And they carry the body into the country with great rejoicings. And they have a great table in readiness, upon which the priests cut off the head, and then this is presented to the son. And the son and all the company raise a chant and make many prayers for the dead. Then the priests cut the whole of the body to pieces, and when they have done so they go up again to the city with the whole company, praying for him as they go. After this the eagles and vultures come down from the mountains and every one takes his morsel and carries it away. Then all the company shout aloud, saying, "Behold! the man is a saint! For the angels of God come and carry him to Paradise." And in this way the son deems himself to be honored in no small degree, seeing that his father is borne off in this creditable manner by the angels. And so he takes his father's head, and straightway cooks it and eats it; and of the skull he maketh a goblet, from which he and all of the family always drink devoutly to the memory of the deceased father. And they say that by acting in this way they show their great respect for their father. And many other preposterous and abominable customs have they.

46. Of a rich man in Manzi, and how he was fed by fifty maidens.

When I was still in the province of Manzi, I passed by the foot of the palace wall of a certain burgess whose manner of life is thus. He hath fifty damsels, virgins, who wait on him continually; and when he goeth to dinner and taketh his seat at table the dishes are brought to him by fives and fives, those virgins carrying them in with singing of songs and the music of many kinds of instruments. And they also feed him as if he were a pet sparrow, putting the food into his mouth, singing before him continually until those dishes be disposed of. Then other five dishes are brought by other five maidens, with other songs and kinds of music, whilst the first maidens retire. And thus he leadeth his life daily until he shall have lived it out. Now this man hath a revenue of 30 tumans of *tagars* of rice. And each tuman is ten thousand, and each *tagar* is the amount of a heavy ass-load. The court of the palace in which he dwells hath an extent of two miles; and the pavement thereof hath one tile of gold and another of silver in turn. And in the said court there is a hill made of gold and silver, upon which are erected monasteries and bell-towers, and the like [in miniature] such as men make for their amusement. And 'tis said that there be four men such as he in the realm of Manzi.

Moreover 'tis the mark of gentility in that country to have the nails long; and some let their thumbnails grow to such an extent that they grow right round the hand. And with the women the great beauty is to have little feet; and for this reason mothers are accustomed, as soon as girls are born to them, to swathe their feet tightly so that they can never grow in the least.

47. Of the Old Man of the Mountain, and his end.

After I had left the lands of Prester John and was travelling towards the west, I came to a certain country which is called Millestorte, a fair and very fertile region. In this country used to dwell a certain one who was called the Old Man of the Mountain.[66] Between two of the mountains of that region he had built a wall, and this he carried right round one of the mountains. And inside this wall were the most delightful fountains of water, and beside them were set the most charming virgins on the face of the earth, as well as splendid horses and everything else that could be thought of for the gratification of man's senses. Wine and milk also were made to flow there by certain conduits; and the place had the name of Paradise.

66. The story of the Old Man of the Mountain, also narrated by Marco Polo, would have taken place in the Persian area, in an autonomous state whose sovereign lived in an inaccessible castle in the Elburz Mountains, a castle destroyed by the Mongols in the second half of the thirteenth century.

And when he found any youth of promise he caused him to be admitted to his Paradise. And then when he desired to cause any king or baron to be assassinated, or poignarded, he called on the officer who was set over that Paradise to select someone who was most fitted for the business, and who most delighted in the life led in that Paradise of his. To this young man a certain potion was given which immediately set him fast asleep, and so in his sleep he was carried forth from that Paradise. And when he awoke again, and found himself no longer in Paradise, he went into such a madness of grief that he knew not what he did. And when he importuned that Old One of the Mountain to let him back again into Paradise, the reply was: "Thither thou canst not return until thou shalt have slain such a king or baron. And then, whether thou live or die, I will bring thee back into Paradise again." And so through the youth's great lust to get back into his Paradise, he got murdered by his hand whomsoever he list. And thus the fear of this Old One was upon all the kings of the East, and they paid him heavy tribute. But when the Tartars had conquered nearly the whole of the East, they came also to the land of that Old Man, and at last took his dominion from him. And when they had done this, he sent forth many of his assassins from his Paradise, and by their hands caused many Tartars to be assassinated and slain. And when the Tartars saw this, they came to the city wherein the Old Man dwelt, and besieged it, and quitted it not until they took it and the Old Man also. Him they bound in chains, and caused to suffer a miserable death.

48. How the friars deal with devils in Tartary.

In those regions God Almighty hath bestowed such grace upon the Minor Friars that in Great Tartary they think it a mere nothing to expel devils from the possessed, no more indeed than to drive a dog out of the house. For there be many in those parts possessed of the devil both men and women, and these they bind and bring to our friars from as far as ten days' journey off. The friars bid the demons depart forth instantly from the bodies of the possessed in the name of Jesus Christ, and they do depart immediately in obedience to this command. Then those who have been delivered from the demon straightway cause themselves to be baptized; and the friars take their idols, which are made of felt, and carry them to the fire, whilst all the people of the country round assemble to see their neighbor's gods burnt. The friars, accordingly, cast the

157

idols into the fire, but they leap out again. And so the friars take holy water and sprinkle it upon the fire, and that straightway drives away the demon from the fire; and so the friars again casting the idols into the fire, they are consumed. And then the devil in the air raises a shout, saying: "See then, see then, how I am expelled from my dwelling-place." And in this way our friars baptize great numbers in that country.

49. The friar telleth of a certain valley wherein he saw terrible things.

Another great and terrible thing I saw. For, as I went through a certain valley[67] which lieth by the River of Delights, I saw therein many dead corpses lying. And I heard also therein sundry kinds of music, but chiefly nakers, or kettledrums, which were marvellously played upon. And so great was the noise thereof that very great fear came

67. This valley has not been identified. According to Yule, the story — even though notably expanded and fictionalized — could have some basis in truth; it could refer to some valley in the Hindu Kush that Odoric perhaps crossed on his return trip.

upon me. Now, this valley is seven or eight miles long; and if any unbeliever enter therein he quitteth it never again, but perisheth incontinently. Yet I hesitated not to go in that I might see once for all what the matter was. And when I had gone in I saw there, as I have said, such numbers of corpses as no one without seeing it could deem credible. And at one side of the valley, in the very rock, I beheld as it were the face of a man very great and terrible, so very terrible indeed that for my exceeding great fear my spirit seemed to die in me. Wherefore I made the sign of the cross, and began continually to repeat *Verbum caro factum* ("The Word became flesh"), but I dared not at all to come nigh that face, but kept at seven or eight paces from it. And so I came at length to the other end of the valley, and there I ascended a hill of sand and looked around me. But nothing could I descry, only I still heard those nakers to play which were played so marvellously. And when I got to the top of that hill I found there a great quantity of silver heaped up as it had been fishes' scales, and some of this I put into my bosom. But as I cared nought for it, and was at the same time in fear lest it should be a snare to hinder my escape, I cast it all down again to the ground. And so by God's grace I came forth unscathed. Then all the Saracens, when they heard of this, showed me great worship, saying that I was a baptized and holy man. But those who had perished in that valley they said belonged to the devil.

50. Friar Odoric attesteth the truth of his story.

I, Friar Odoric the Bohemian[68] of Friuli, from a certain town called Pordenone, of the Order of Minorites and the province of St. Anthony, do solemnly declare and attest to my reverend father the Friar Guidotto, the minister of the province aforesaid of St. Anthony in the March of Treviso, in accordance with my vow of obedience and the injunction which he hath laid upon me, that all these things hereinbefore written I either beheld with mine own eyes or heard from men worthy of credit. And as for such things as I saw not myself, the common talk of those countries beareth witness to their truth. And many things I have left out and have not caused to be written lest they should be deemed too hard for belief by such as have not seen them with their own eyes. But, as for me, from day to

68. The appellative "The Bohemian," which Yule approved, is found in only one of the manuscripts of the *Relatio*.

day I prepare myself to return to those countries in which I am content to die, if so it pleaseth Him from whom all good things do come.

Now, all the things hereinbefore contained were faithfully taken down in writing by Friar William of Solagna, just as the aforenamed Friar Odoric the Bohemian uttered them, in the year of the Lord M.CCC.XXX, in the month of May, and at the house of St. Anthony in Padua. Nor did he trouble himself to adorn the matter with difficult Latin and conceits of style, but just as the other told his story so Friar William wrote it, so that all may understand the more easily what is told herein.

51. Friar Marchesino of Bassano addeth his say; and telleth a pretty passage that he heard of Odoric.

I, Friar Marchesino of Bassano, of the Order of Minorites, desire to say that I heard the preceding relations from the aforesaid Friar Odoric when he was still living; and I heard a good deal more which he has not set down. Among other stories which he told, this was one:[69]

69. Two different versions of this story exist: that narrated by

He related that once upon a time, when the Great Khan was on his journey from Sandu to Cambalech, he (Friar Odoric), with four other Minor Friars, was sitting under the shade of a tree by the side of the road along which the Khan was about to pass. And one of the brethren was a bishop. So when the Khan began to draw near, the bishop put on his episcopal robes and took a cross and fastened it to the end of a staff, so as to raise it aloft; and then those four began to chant with loud voices the hymn, *Veni Creator Spiritus!*[70] And then the Great Khan, hearing the sound thereof, asked what it meant. And those four barons who go beside him replied that it was four of the Frank Rabbans (i.e., of the Christian monks). So the Khan called them to him, and the bishop thereupon taking the cross from the staff presented it to the Khan to kiss. Now at the time he was lying down, but as soon as he saw the cross he sat up, and doffing the cap that he wore, kissed the cross in the most reverent and humble manner. Now, the rule and custom of that court is that no one shall ven-

---

Brother Marchesino of Bassano, reported here, and that which is generally incorporated into William of Solagna's account.

70. "Come Creator Spirit!" — a hymn to the Holy Spirit used by the Catholic Church in the solemn liturgy of major festivals.

ture to come into the Khan's presence empty-handed. So Friar Odoric, having with him a small dish full of apples, presented that as their offering to the Great Khan. And he took two of the apples, and ate a piece of one of them whilst he kept the other in his hand, and so he went his way.

Now, it is clear enough from this that the Khan himself had some savor of our Catholic faith, as he well might through the Minor Friars who dwell at his court continually. And as for that cap which he doffed so reverently before the cross, I have heard Friar Odoric say that it was a mass of pearls and gems, and was worth more than the whole March of Treviso.

52. The blessed end of Friar Odoric.[71]

Now, the blessed man Odoric, after he had come back from foreign parts to his own province, to wit, the March of Treviso, became desirous of visiting the Supreme Pontiff, in order to obtain leave from him to take away with

71. The final chapter in Yule's report is taken from the edition of the *Relatio* re-elaborated by the Bohemian Franciscan Henry of Glarus.

him again a body of fifty friars, no matter from what province, provided they had the will to go. So he departed from Friuli, the district of his birth. But when he got to Pisa he was seized with a sore illness which forced him to return to his own province. And so it was that in Udine, a city of Friuli, in the year of the Lord's Incarnation M.CCC.XXXI, and the day before the Ides of January, he passed triumphantly from this world to the glories of the blessed. And his virtues and miraculous powers have been there most brilliantly displayed. For through his means the blind, the lame, the dumb, the deaf, are, by the Lord's permission, made perfectly whole. Glory to God, Amen!

INDEX